BERLITZ®

MOROCCO

- A ✔ in the text denotes a highly recommended sight
- A complete A-Z of practical information starts on p.107
- Extensive mapping throughout: on cover flaps and in text

Although we make every effort to ensure the accuracy of the information in this guide, changes do occur. If you have any new information, suggestions or corrections to contribute to the guide, we would like to hear from you. Please write to Berlitz Publishing at one of the above addresses.

Text: Neil Wilson
Editors: Jane Middleton, Delphine Verroest
Photography: Chris Coe
Layout: Suzanna Boyle
Cartography: Visual Image
Thanks to: The Office National Marocain du Tourisme

Cover photograph: *A Moroccan brick arch* © The Image Bank
Photograph on page 4: *Fès – view from the Merenid Tombs*

CONTENTS

Morocco and the Moroccans

Morocco is only a three-hour flight from London or a one-hour ferry trip from Spain, and yet it is as exotic and exciting a destination as any in the Far East or Latin America.

Morocco assaults the traveller with a barrage of new sensations – sights, sounds and scents seem more intense, and the atmosphere more charged. From the rich gold of Essaouira's battlements basking in the setting sun to the deep blue shadows in the snowfields of the High Atlas, and from the rich, deep scarlet of newly dyed wool in the souks of Fès to the cool green shade of the cypress forests around Ifrane, the colours seem brighter and more vibrant. The tang of orange blossom on a city street and the sensuous smells of leather and sandalwood present in the markets of Marrakech, the pungent aromas of cumin and coriander and the whiff of incense wafting from a Medina doorway, are scents more rich and mysterious than anything else you might experience back home.

Although a mere 20km (12 miles) separate the Spanish and Moroccan coasts, as soon as you set foot in Morocco you know – and feel – you have left Europe far behind.

The kingdom of Morocco lies at the northwestern corner of the African continent, facing Europe across the narrow Strait of Gibraltar. It stretches for roughly 2,000km (1,240 miles) from the Mediterranean coast at Tangier to the sands of the Sahara at Laayoune. Most of the country is occupied by the Atlas Mountains, which run southwest from the Algerian border to the Atlantic coast, isolating the coastal plain from the rest of Africa. Its physical isolation is one reason why Morocco was the only part of North Africa to remain uncolonized until the 20th century.

This is a land of tremendous variety. The jagged limestone peaks of the Rif Mountains to the southeast of Tangier give way to the cultivated coastal

Moroccan artisans are renowned throughout the world for their meticulous craftsmanship.

plains that lie between Rabat and Casablanca and the foothills of the Atlas Mountains. These mountains are rugged, but lack any really spectacular peaks, forming instead a series of long ridges, reaching a height of 4,167m (13,670ft) in Djébel Toubkal, which is the **6** highest point in North Africa.

South of the Atlas, the landscape is dry and desolate, as befits the fringes of the Sahara, but enlivened with colourful rock outcrops, and the green splashes of date palm oases.

As with the landscape, so with the climate. The coast from Tangier to Agadir enjoys a temperate climate, averaging around 15°C (60°F) in winter and 25°C (75°F) in summer; rainfall is concentrated in the north, and falls mainly in winter; the southern beach resort of Agadir can boast 300 days of sunshine a year. The inland cities of Fès and Meknès are slightly cooler in winter and warmer in summer, but it is in the mountains that the most extreme variations are to be found. On the summit ridges of the Atlas, temperatures can plummet to -20°C (-8°F) in midwinter, and soar to a searing 40°C (105°F) in summer when the desert winds blow from the east.

The population of Morocco is around 26 million, concentrated in the coastal plains and especially around Casablanca, Rabat and Tangier. The people are a mixture of the aboriginal Berbers, and the Arabs who invaded the region in the 7th century. Although the races are now well mixed, there is still a considerable number of full-blooded Berbers in the remote mountain areas, where a quarter of the population can speak only their native Berber tongue. Physically they are quite different from the dark-eyed Arabs, with reddish hair and most striking blue or green eyes. In the far south you will meet the Tuareg, the nomadic tribesmen of the Sahara, easily recognized by their dark skins and dark blue robes.

This huge and varied country is unified by Islam, the national religion, headed by the king, who is the spiritual leader of the community. Like all Muslims, Moroccans must adhere to the principles known as

In Morocco life moves at a slower pace, and there is time to rest in the shade and chat.

'The Five Pillars of Islam': to accept that 'there is no God but God, and Mohammed is his Prophet'; to pray five times daily, at dawn, midday, afternoon, sunset and after dark; to give alms to the poor and contribute to the upkeep of the mosques; to fast between sunrise and sunset during Rama-dan; and to try to make the pilgrimage (hadj) to Mecca at least once.

Moroccans are by nature friendly and welcoming, and proud of their heritage – don't be discouraged by the touts and hustlers who hang around the more popular tourist attractions. In the countryside especially you will encounter genuine hospitality and a real

*T*raditional Moroccan occupations – a Marrakech water-seller and a goatherd near Goulimine.

8

interest in your travels. You will often be offered a glass of mint tea – a long-established custom and a mark of friendship – asked where you come from and where you are going, and much pleasure will be taken in answering your own questions about the village, its crafts and its customs.

Far too many visitors miss out on the best of Morocco by sticking to the popular package-holiday resorts of Tangier and Agadir. Make the effort to explore a little further afield and you will be rewarded with an experience every bit as exciting as the more expensive attractions of exotic long-haul destinations. As you will find out, the true magic of Morocco reveals itself only to the traveller with a sense of adventure.

A Brief History

Morocco is a vast and varied territory, only recently united into a modern nation state. Its long history records a struggle for ascendancy among the Berber tribes of the mountains and the Arabs of the plains, the rise and fall of powerful dynasties, the creation and collapse of mighty empires and, from the 18th century onward, manipulation and exploitation by European powers seeking to expand their empires.

The ancient Greeks called this land the country of Atlas, the Titan who was condemned by Zeus to bear the heavens upon his shoulders. Here, at the western extremity of their world, where the chariot of the sun god Helios vanished over the horizon each night and the Hesperides, or Daughters of Evening, tended their magical garden, Atlas watched over his huge herds of sheep and cattle.

According to legend, however, the hero Perseus showed him the head of the gorgon Medusa to punish him for his inhospitality, and Atlas was transformed into the mountain range that still bears his name.

The Phoenicians were the first to explore this far western land, setting up a trading post at Liks (Lixus) on the Moroccan coast around 1000BC. In the succeeding centuries they and their descendants, the Carthaginians, founded many such outposts, including those at Tangier and Essaouira, while also building a town at the site of present-day Rabat. They called the fierce inhabitants of the interior *barbaros*, whose meaning, 'not of our people', persisted through the ages as 'Berber'. (The English word 'barbarian' has the same root.)

The origins of the Berbers remain a mystery. Some theories link them with the Celts, the Basques and even the Canaanites, but it is far more likely that they are descendants of the Neolithic Capsian culture, which spread through North Africa in the 5th and 6th millennia BC. Berbers have preserved their own languages and traditional customs right down to the present day.

HISTORICAL LANDMARKS

c. 1000BC   Phoenician sailors build trading posts along coast.

146BC   Carthage falls to Rome. Northern Morocco included in province of Mauretania.

3rd-4th cen. AD   Decline and fall of Roman Empire; withdrawal from Morocco.

683   Muslim conquest of Morocco under Oqba ibn Nafi.

711   The Moors launch their conquest of Spain.

788-926   Idrissid dynasty: Moulay Idriss II founds Fès.

1062-1147   Almoravid dynasty: nomad conquerors from the South. Marrakech founded in 1602 by Yusuf ibn Tashfin. In 1103, Almoravid Empire stretches from Marrakech to northeastern Spain.

1147   Almohad armies take Fès and Marrakech.

1130-1269   Almohad dynasty. From 1163 to1212, Almohad Empire includes Morocco, Algeria, Tunisia, Libya and Spain.

1244-1398   Merinid dynasty: the last Berber dynasty.

1248   Merinids seize power in Fès; Almohads surrender at Marrakech in 1269.

15th cen.   Anarchy reigns. End of Muslim Empire in Spain.

1548-1659   Saadian dynasty: masters of Marrakech. Portuguese defeated at Battle of Three Kings in 1578.

1666-pres.   Alaouite dynasty – national revival.

1672   Moulay Ismaïl builds his Imperial City at Meknès.

1912   Franco-Spanish Protectorate established in Morocco.

1956   Morocco granted independence.

1962   King Hassan II ascends to the throne.

1975   'Green March' into the Spanish Sahara.

1989   Morocco joins with its North African neighbours to form the Arab Maghreb Union.

*T*his bronze of Berber King Juba II was found amid the ruins of Roman Volubilis.

All through the 3rd and 4th centuries BC, Berber kingdoms were established in many parts of Morocco. From these small strongholds, over a thousand years later, the Berber people were to build mighty empires which ruled all of North Africa and most of Spain. First, however, came the Romans.

Roman Morocco

When Carthage fell in 146BC, North Africa became part of the Roman Empire. The western province of Mauretania Tingitana occupied the northern parts of Morocco and Algeria, with the town of Tingis (present-day Tangier) as its capital. From 25BC to AD23 Mauretania was ruled by Juba II, a handsome young Berber king installed by the Emperor Augustus. A fine scholar, Juba was educated in Rome and made journeys to countries as far away as Arabia to gather material for the many books he wrote. His wife, Cleopatra Selene, was the daughter of Mark Antony and Cleopatra. A fine bronze statue of Juba II, found at the site of Volubilis, is on display at the Archaeological Museum in Rabat.

The Roman Empire made few inroads into Morocco itself, concentrating its attention on the richer lands of Africa Proconsularis (Tunisia), so the language and culture of the mountain Berbers was little affected by Roman civilization.

The Muslim Conquest

The 7th century saw the rise of Islam in Arabia. In the early years believers were organized into a small, close-knit community headed by the Prophet Mohammed himself. However, as more and more people embraced the new faith, the community of Islam grew rapidly, and armies were raised to spread the word, using force where necessary. Within a century of Mohammed's death in AD632, the Muslim armies had conquered the whole of the Middle East including Persia (Iran), all of North Africa, and parts of Spain and France.

Among the Arab generals were many great leaders, one of whom, the mighty Oqba ibn Nafi, founded the holy city of Kairouan in Tunisia in 670. (He also built North Africa's first mosque.) From Kairouan, in 683, Oqba led his raiding armies all the way to the Atlantic coast of Morocco. Legend has it that he then rode his horse into the surf, proclaiming that only the ocean could prevent him from advancing even further. He also named the land Al Maghrib al-Aksa, Arabic for 'The Far West'.

Having done so, he turned and headed south, leading his armies to the old Roman capital of Volubilis. From there he marched to what is now Marrakech and on to Agadir, and then even further south to the fringes of the desert. Here in southern Morocco he had several skirmishes with tribes of nomadic Berbers who wore rough cloths across their faces to protect them from the desert sands. Little could the general know that one day these veiled men of the desert would rule all the lands he had so recently conquered.

Oqba ibn Nafi was killed by an old adversary on his return march to Arabia, but over the next 30 years other dauntless commanders followed in his footsteps. The native Berbers embraced Islam with enthusiasm and joined the crusading armies, crossing the Strait of Gibraltar to carry the banner of Islam into Spain and France. For the next six centuries, the Islamic civilization of Spain **13** and Morocco outshone that of the Christian world.

The history of the country from the time of the Muslim Conquest is a tale of dynasty succeeding dynasty. After consolidating power, subduing enemies and building imposing cities, mosques and palaces, each regime would slide into decadence – leading to weak government, political chaos and bitter fighting, until a new faction stepped in to fill the power vacuum.

The Idrissids

As it stood, the Islamic Empire was spread too thin and contained too many peoples to last long as a single entity. Soon

The holy town of Moulay Idriss is framed by a Roman archway at Volubilis, the ancient Roman capital.

many regions were governed by princes and potentates, especially in the vast and fragmented territories of Morocco.

Nothing was better proof of nobility than being a *sharif*, a descendant of the Prophet Mohammed. One such was Moulay Idriss, who arrived in Volubilis in 788 and was proclaimed king by the chief of the local Berber tribes. As a descendant of the Prophet he possessed great *baraka* (divine blessing), which brought good fortune to his followers, and consequently his power and influence grew rapidly.

His success didn't go without alarming Harun al Rashid, the powerful Caliph of Baghdad, who despatched an assassin with a phial of poison to insinuate himself into Idriss's group of followers. The poison did its work. Moulay Idriss was buried near the city of Volubilis, and the village that contains his tomb (and still bears his name) is one of the most sacred Muslim shrines in all Morocco (see p.54).

His son, Moulay Idriss II, founded an impressive capital for the Idrissid Empire at Fès, not far from the Roman city of Volubilis (see p.52). His city was built around the area now occupied by the great Karaouine Mosque, and its population was swelled by refugees from the great Islamic cities of Kairouan in Tunisia and Cordoba in Spain, adding to its cultural and spiritual life.

Idriss II died in 828, and his empire was split between his eight sons. This led to a weakening of the state and rebellion among the tribes, paving the way for a new regime.

The Almoravids

The next Moroccan dynasty had its origins among the Berber tribes of the desert regions – the 'veiled ones' encountered by Oqba ibn Nafi just three centuries earlier (see p.13). A young Muslim religious student named Abdallah ibn Yasin came south from the region of Agadir to preach to the Berbers, and soon emerged as a spirited and vigorous leader. His teachings were based on the strictest discipline, and **15** missing prayers was punished with a severe whipping. Even the Berbers, accustomed to the hardships of life in the Sahara, found Ibn Yasin's regime too harsh, and he and his band of followers were soon pushed south across the desert. They then built themselves a fortified monastery, called a *ribat*, on the sub-Saharan coast in Mauritania, and created a community of religious warriors, quite similar to the Christian Knights of the Crusades (the name Almoravid comes from the Arabic *al Murabitun*, 'people of the ribat').

Between 1054 and 1059 a small army of these puritans swept northwards through the land and conquered southern Morocco, wrecking drinking places, smashing musical instruments, and imposing their strict religious code. In 1056 they took Taroudannt, and in 1062 founded the city of Marrakech as their headquarters.

Despite their violent fanaticism, it was the Almoravids who initiated the golden age of Moroccan art and culture. As they advanced northwards through Morocco, these unsophisticated nomads picked up many of the more civilized customs of the other Berbers and the Arabs. In 1086 when they received a plea for help from the Muslim rulers of the Spanish Kingdom, who were in trouble from Christian at-

*T*he Karaouine Mosque in Fès was built by the Almoravids in the late 9th century.

tacks, the Almoravids flooded into Spain under the leadership of the great Yusuf ibn Tashfin. Yusuf soon became the most powerful Muslim ruler in all Spain and the Maghreb.

His soldiers acquired many of the habits and appetites of the dissolute but highly cultured Muslim civilization of Andalusia, and the richness of Moorish art and architecture soon spread throughout Morocco, and especially in Yusuf's southern stronghold of Marrakech, which took over from Fès as the principal city of Morocco. Though the older city gave up its primacy, the Almoravids graced it with the dazzlingly splendid Karaouine Mosque (see p.60).

The Almohads

The powerful Yusuf ibn Tashfin died in 1107. Some years later a young Moroccan theological student travelled east to visit the prestigious Muslim colleges of the Arabian heartland. Fired with religious fervour, Mohammed ibn Tumart returned to Morocco and began a conservative reforming movement much like that of the early Almoravids, preaching absolute unity with God. (The name Almohad comes, in fact, from the Arabic *al Muwahhidun* meaning 'the Unitarians'.)

Ibn Tumart was a religious fanatic who soon made himself very unpopular with local officials. On one occasion he even disrupted a wedding procession, shouting vociferously 'Women should walk!' as he forced the bride from the saddle, and smashing to bits all the merrymakers' musical instruments. Though Ibn Tumart received many forceful admonitions to mind his own business, he also acquired a large following of religious zealots. Together they imitated the example of the early Almoravids and withdrew to a fortress-monastery at Tinmal, in the High Atlas mountains between Marrakech and Taroudannt.

Ibn Tumart died in 1130 and his right-hand man, Abd el Moumen, carried on the crusade. However, Abd el Moumen was more warrior than **17** preacher, and proved an outstanding general. In two campaigns between 1151 and 1159 he displaced the Almoravids and seized control of all North Africa, eventually taking over Muslim Spain as well. The Almohad Empire lasted for over a century, and during the reign of Yacoub el Mansour ('The Conqueror', grandson of Abd el Moumen) it brought Moroccan power and civilization to one of its peaks. Almohad rule extended from Morocco to Algeria and Tunisia through to Libya, and deep into Spain.

The Moorish culture of Andalusia seduced the Almohads as it had the earlier Almoravids; some of the most beautiful monuments of Islamic art were created under their reign. The influence of Spanish Muslim art can be found in the masterpieces of Almohad architecture in Morocco – the Koutoubia Minaret in Marrakech (see p.73), and the Hassan Tower and Oudaïa Kasbah Gate in Rabat (see p.37).

Having achieved ascendancy, the Almohad rulers then **18** succumbed to the nigh inevit-

able decadence, and their grip on power weakened. Anarchy reigned in Marrakech, while warring clans battled for control of Moroccan territory.

The Merinids

Another Berber dynasty, the Beni Merin from the eastern steppes near Taza, seized power in Fès in 1248. Their motive was not religious zeal but simple greed for land, power, riches and privileges. By the time they took Marrakech in 1269, the whole country had fallen under their sway.

A hundred years of Merinid rule brought glory to Fès, just as Almohad rule had to Marrakech. To embellish their imperial capital, the Merinids constructed the 'new' city of Fès el Jédid, and also built the two most exquisite *medersas* (religious colleges) in the old city, the el Attarîn (from 1325) and the Bou Inania (1355). The tombs of the Merinid kings, in ruins today, still dominate Fès from a nearby hill. In Rabat, the massive Chellah was their fortified cemetery, and in Spain the magnificent Alhambra Palace in Granada was built during their reign.

The demise of the Merinids in the 15th century saw the end of Berber domination of Morocco. The empire crumbled into chaos at the hands of incompetent rulers while Christian Europe was entering the Renaissance. The power of the Christian princes grew as their wealth and scientific knowledge increased. Christian warships and pirates attacked the Moroccan coasts. By the early 1500s, Portugal held most of the important towns along the Atlantic coast of Morocco, and later in the century the Spaniards took over Sebta (Ceuta).

The Hassan Tower is one of the great masterpieces of Almohad architecture.

The Saadians

The Saadi dynasty was a clan of Arab origin descended from the Prophet Mohammed, who surged northward from their homeland in the Drâa valley to confront the Christian invaders. They took Agadir from the Portuguese in 1541, and by 1576 had installed themselves in Fès as the new rulers of Morocco. In 1578 they defeated the Portuguese in the famous Battle of the Three Kings, and extended their empire southwards to Timbuktu in Mali, where they traded in gold, sugar and slaves. Marrakech was their favoured city, and under the reign of King Ahmed el Mansour (1578-1603), known **19**

*T*he richly decorated tomb of Moulay Ismaïl lies within the Imperial City of Meknès.

as Edh Dhahabi (or 'The Golden One'), they lavished their considerable wealth on monu-

20 ments such as the palace of El Badi and the exquisite Saadian Tombs (see p.77).

Following the death of King Ahmed in 1603, the dynasty fragmented, and the great age of medieval Moroccan independence was past. The early 17th century found the Saadians reposing peacefully in the glorious tombs they had built for themselves in Marrakech.

The Alaouites

A brand new national leadership emerged with the Alaouite dynasty, who came from the oases of the Tafilalet, on the edge of the Sahara south of Erfoud. They were invited by the people of Fès to bring order to the country. By 1672 the Alaouites had control of Marrakech, and the notorious sultan Moulay Ismaïl (1672-1727) had come to power.

Moulay Ismaïl was a man with powerful appetites (it is said he fathered over a thousand children) and a thirst for glory. A cruel and ruthless tyrant, Ismaïl nevertheless succeeded in uniting much of the country and bringing it to the attention of Europe. Forsaking the Moroccan imperial cities of Marrakech and Fès, he built his own imperial city at Meknès, where he entertained foreign ambassadors in a luxury that rivalled that of Versailles.

After the death of Moulay Ismaïl, Morocco once again slumped into several decades of anarchy and privation. Other capable Alaouite monarchs came to the throne in the late 18th century, but by that time the Christian countries of Europe were looking to Africa to expand their empires, a threat emphasized by the French seizure of Algiers in 1830.

A Franco-Spanish Protectorate

Resourceful Alaouite sultans successfully played off one European power against another throughout the 19th century, but the odds against them increased progressively, with France, Spain, Germany and Britain all attempting to influence events to their own advantage – and with France in particular playing an increasingly important role in Moroccan affairs.

Morocco gradually became more and more dependent on French military protection, and the Treaty of Fès in 1912 made it into a Franco-Spanish Protectorate, with its capital in Rabat. The French, under the far-sighted, able administration of Marshal Lyautey, governed the central and southern parts of the country. Spain controlled the northernmost portion except for Tangier, which became an International Zone.

The Protectorate did bring some of the hallmarks of the Western world to Moroccan life – roads and railways were built, a modern education system was established, and new towns (*villes nouvelles*) were built alongside the old Medinas, while agriculture and mining were also encouraged.

These were turbulent years, however, and for the young Moroccans growing up in the 1920s, progress was worthless without independence.

The young crown prince of the Alaouite dynasty, who in 1927 was chosen by the French **21** as sultan, sympathized in silence with them, but was in no position to act.

Independence

France's hold on Morocco was weakened during World War II, and Moroccan nationalists came out in the open to form the Istiqlal (Independence) Party. The young sultan, Mohammed V, was firmly on their side, but he had to tread carefully lest the Protectorate took action against him. After World War II, in an attempt to suppress the nationalist party, the French exiled Mohammed V and his family to Corsica and then Madagascar. This plan backfired by making the sultan a popular symbol of courage and resistance to foreign rule.

By 1955 the French were forced to recall the royal hero from his house arrest abroad. He was hailed as the saviour of his country, and saw his efforts rewarded by the granting of independence in March 1956. Morocco was once again united under the independent rule of an Alaouite sultan.

Mohammed V, who changed his title from 'sultan' to 'king', had just embarked upon his ambitious plans for progress and development when he died in 1961, after a minor operation. The nation was shocked at the untimely passing of the greatest Alaouite sovereign since Moulay Ismaïl. He retains a very special place in the hearts of all Moroccans, who regularly come to pay their respects at his splendid mausoleum in Rabat (see p.38). The main street in just about every town in the country is named after him.

His son ascended the throne as King Hassan II, and introduced a new constitution. This declared Morocco to be 'a social, democratic and constitutional monarchy'.

Parliamentary elections are held every six years, but power remains largely in the hands of the king. As a *sharif*, he is not only the king but the Emir el Muminin (Commander of the Faithful), or the country's religious leader. Although King Hassan maintains Morocco's age-old traditions, he is a thor-

The much-loved King Mohammed V lies at rest in his splendid mausoleum in Rabat

oughly modern head of state, moderate, progressive, and a friend of the West.

One of the most momentous events of King Hassan's reign was the so-called *Marche Verte* (Green March) of November 1975, when he led 350,000 unarmed civilians on a march into the former Spanish colony of Western Sahara to assert Moroccan sovereignty over the region. The occupation was resisted by the guerrillas of the Popular Front for the Liberation of Saguia el Hamra and Rio de Oro (better known as the Polisario) but by 1987 Hassan had succeeded in controlling the rebels with a quite remarkable 2,000km (1,250-mile) long defensive sand wall around the new territory.

In 1989, Morocco, Algeria, Tunisia, Libya and Mauretania joined together to form the Arab Maghreb Union, which led to closer economic and diplomatic ties between the countries, as well as an easing of border controls. The union resulted in the withdrawal of Algerian backing for the Polisario, followed by a UN-controlled cease-fire imposed in the Western Sahara. The Polisario suffered another huge setback when its leader defected to Morocco in 1992, and the round of talks between the rebels and the Moroccan government in 1993 failed to resolve the conflict.

23

Where to Go

Morocco is a huge country, extending over 2,000km (some 1,250 miles) from Tangier to the southern border with Mauritania, but fortunately for the visitor the main tourist attractions are concentrated in the northern third, between Tangier and Agadir. It would be impossible to see all that Morocco has to offer in a single trip, so it pays to be selective – our list of highlights on the opposite page should help.

Top of the list for most first-time visitors must be Morocco's four magnificent Imperial Cities – Fès, Meknès, Rabat and Marrakech. It's here that the splendour and magnificence of past Moroccan empires are concentrated. The independent traveller can easily reach them all by train or bus, but if you plan to set off and explore south of Marrakech, a hire car will prove very useful (see p.110).

The point of arrival for the great majority of package tourists, and for most people taking the ferry from Spain or Gibraltar, is Tangier. This is where we start our tour of Morocco, too.

Tangier (*Tanger*)

Located at the northern tip of Morocco, where Africa and Europe face each other across the Strait of Gibraltar, Tangier has always held a rather special position in Moroccan history. The Phoenicians set up a trading post here, and later the Romans founded the town of Tingis, which lent its name to the whole province of Mauretania Tingitana.

Succeeding centuries saw it fall under Vandal, Byzantine, Arab, Moroccan, Spanish and Portuguese rule; for a brief period (1662-84) it belonged to England, as part of the dowry of the Portuguese Catherine of Braganza, the bride of Charles II. Under British rule, extensive fortifications were erected.

After the Protectorate was established in 1912 (see p.21) Tangier was granted special status as an International Zone.

HIGHLIGHTS OF MOROCCO

Atlas Mountains. Snow-capped mountain range to the south of Marrakech provides superb trekking country, and is crossed by two scenic passes, the Tizi n'Test and Tizi n'Tichka. (See pp.79 and 85)

Dadès and Todra Gorges. These spectacular ravines on the south side of the Atlas Mountains can boast some of Morocco's most impressive scenery. (See p.87)

Drâa Valley. Stretching southwards from the desert outpost of Ouarzazate, this dramatic valley offers spectacular scenery, ancient *ksour* (fortified villages), and lush date palm oases on the edge of the Sahara Desert. (See p.85)

Essaouira. This fortified harbour town, built over 200 years ago, is Morocco's most attractive coastal resort, famous for its battlements, its woodworkers and its windsurfing. (See p.83)

Grand Mosque of Hassan II, Casablanca. The world's biggest mosque outside of Mecca. Its 210m (690ft) high minaret is topped with a green laser beam pointing to the east. (See p.44)

Jemaa el Fna, Marrakech. Like a scene from *The Arabian Nights*, this square provides a nightly stage for all manner of musicians, dancers, acrobats, storytellers and magicians. The square is dominated by the graceful Koutoubia Minaret, the city's most prominent landmark. (See p.73)

Mausoleum of Mohammed V, Rabat. This magnificently decorated monument is dedicated to the ruler who gained independence for Morocco. Opposite the mausoleum rises the 12th-century Hassan Tower, one of the architectural glories of the Almohad dynasty. (See pp.38 and 39)

Medina of Fès el Bali. The oldest of Morocco's four Imperial Cities, a living example of a medieval town, now a World Heritage Site. (See p.58)

Saadian Tombs, Marrakech. Sumptuously decorated necropolis of the Saadian dynasty, which lay undisturbed from the 17th century until 1917. (See p.77)

It was governed by a commission of foreign diplomats, and this peculiar arrangement – together with the city's special privileges as a free port – attracted many European and American expatriates and adventurers. Although Tangier today is as much a part of Morocco as Rabat or Marrakech, it does retain a cosmopolitan flavour quite distinct from the rest of the country.

During the Protectorate northern Morocco was governed by Spain, and Spanish predominates over French as the second language of many inhabitants; you'll hear *buenos días* more often than *bonjour*.

VILLE NOUVELLE

The first view of Morocco for ferry passengers arriving from Spain is the white houses of Tangier spilling and tumbling down the steep hillside below the kasbah, with the golden sands of the Bay of Tangier stretching away to the east.

Like all Moroccan cities, Tangier consists of a walled Medina, or old town, as well as a modern quarter built during the Protectorate, called the Ville Nouvelle (New Town). At the centre of the Ville Nouvelle lie the main square of Place de France and the tree-lined main street, Boulevard Pasteur, lined with busy cafés, crowded restaurants, news-stands and travel agencies. The

Beautiful beaches and lively cafés pull in the crowds in cosmopolitan Tangier.

27

Modern television aerials sprout from ancient rooftops in Tangier's Medina.

terrace off the square along Boulevard Pasteur has a fine view of the harbour and the Spanish mainland, just 27km (17 miles) away, and is a favourite gathering-place in the evenings for tourists and *tangerinos* alike.

The Rue de la Liberté (or **28** Zankat el Houria) leads down to the old market place of the **Grand Socco**, at the entrance to Tangier's Medina. Officially called Place du 9 Avril 1947, the Grand Socco is now the terminus for city buses, and has a large taxi rank.

THE MEDINA

The Medina is a maze of narrow streets, passages and blind alleys on the hillside above the harbour. As it is not all that large, perhaps the best way to explore it is simply to wander at random. The Rue es-Siaghin (or Silversmiths' Street) leads from the Grand Socco to the **Petit Socco**, a pleasant open square lined with several attractive cafés. Take a seat and relax with a glass of mint tea, as you watch the colourful crowds passing by.

Make your way uphill to the 17th-century **kasbah**, the fortified precinct that occupies the highest point in the Medina, perched on a clifftop overlooking the sea. The Alaouite sultan, Moulay Ismaïl, chose to build himself a palace here, defended by the batteries of cannon that still bristle today on the ramparts.

Today the palace, called the **Dar el Makhzen**, houses the **Museum of Moroccan Arts**, containing treasures such as illuminated Korans, fine textiles, delicate wood and metal work, Berber carpets, jewellery and ceramics. The adjoining Museum of Antiquities is concerned with aspects of Tangier's history.

At the entrance to the main part of the palace is the former treasury, the **Bit el Mal**. Several rooms, with a balcony overlooking the *méchouar* (parade ground), house the sultan's gigantic wooden strongboxes – they were once filled with gold and precious gems.

Cross the *méchouar* to the observation point for a spectacular view across the strait to Gibraltar and Spain, a mere 20km (12 miles) away.

Women in the traditional dress of the Rif Mountains throng the souks of Tangier.

29

Excursions from Tangier

ASILAH AND LIXUS

Along the road to Rabat, 45km (28 miles) south of Tangier, lies the charming town of **Asilah**. Just off the main road and right on the beach, Asilah is a picture-postcard Atlantic fishing port, complete with an impressive kasbah. Each July the town hosts an international festival, one of the highlights of the cultural year.

Asilah was captured in 1471 by the Portuguese, who built the impressive walls and bastions that enclose the Medina. Spanish occupation followed the Portuguese, and it was not until the end of the 17th century that Sultan Moulay Ismaïl recaptured the town for Morocco. Around the beginning of the 20th century, Asilah was the stronghold of a notorious brigand named Raissouli. At the height of his power, this Moroccan tyrant built himself a palace within the kasbah walls, overlooking the sea. He is said to have forced criminals to fling themselves from the topmost palace windows on to the rocks 30m (100ft) below.

The palace is open during the festival, but remains closed to visitors the rest of the year. The Medina is worth exploring at any time, as colourful painted murals adorn the walls of the houses.

Just outside the town walls, down by the sea, are several small seafood restaurants, with tables on the street and in a garden. The daily catch, fresh from the boats in the nearby harbour, is served up for lunch with a minimum of ceremony and a maximum of flavour. North of the harbour, Asilah's splendid beach stretches almost halfway to Tangier.

Another 38km (24 miles) south of Asilah lie the ruins of ancient **Lixus**, one of the oldest cities in Morocco. The first settlement to be built here, a

*A*tlantic sea breezes cool the brightly painted backstreets of Asilah's Medina.

Phoenician trading post, may have been established as early as the 11th century BC. It was an important centre for the Roman province of Mauretania Tingitana, and it grew rich shipping salt and fish to the capital city of Tingis (Tangier). The remains of the fish-salting factories are right down by the highway. Several temples, baths and a theatre make up the acropolis, right at the top of the hill.

CHAOUEN (Chechaouen/ Chefchaouen/Xaouen)

One of the most memorable excursions you can make from Tangier is to Chaouen, 120km (75 miles) away, high in the Rif Mountains.

On the way, a short detour leads to **Tetouan**, some 60km (38 miles) south of Tangier, strikingly situated on a steep hillside. The town was a major settlement area for Moorish exiles from late 15th-century Spain, expelled after the Christian Reconquest, and later became the capital of Spanish

Rows of olive trees punctuate the rich farmland in the hills near Chaouen.

Morocco during the Protectorate; it retains a distinctly Spanish flavour even to this day. Tetouanis proudly call their city 'the daughter of Granada'. The main attraction for tourists is the charming Medina, with crowded souks and tiny, vine-trellised squares – in stark contrast to the Spanish new town, built on a formal grid of streets. The Medina also harbours an arts museum and an archaeological museum.

The road to the city of Chaouen climbs, twisting and turning, into the Rif Mountains; you turn a corner, and suddenly there it is, clinging to the mountainside, with rocky peaks and precipitous valleys all around. (Chaouen, meaning 'the horns', owes its name to the twin peaks between which it seems to hang.)

Like Tetouan, the town was built by 15th-century Muslim

refugees from Andalusia. It was established as a fortress for the faith, capable of resisting any assaults from nearby Portuguese redoubts. However, until the Spanish arrived in 1920, this remote mountain fastness had remained closed to the world for centuries – only three Europeans had ever succeeded in reaching it.

Red tile roofs and Moorish arches recall Chaouen's Spanish heritage. The main square in the Medina is Place Outa el Hammam, lined with tiny shops and cafés. On one side is the centuries-old **kasbah**, recently restored, and housing a little museum. Its colourful gardens, planted with palm trees and flowers, are a haven of tranquillity.

The country around Chaouen provides excellent hiking – steep green foothills covered with fields and orchards and small, white, tin-roofed houses surround the town, with rocky mountains rising steeply behind. A 3km (2-mile) walk upstream from town leads to the waterfall of **Ras el-Ma**, a lovely picnic spot.

Rabat

The capital city of modern Morocco lies at the mouth of the Bou Regreg river. The site was probably occupied by the Phoenicians as early as the 8th century BC, and the Romans built their southernmost port, Sala Colonia, here in the 1st century AD. But it was not until the 10th century that a local Berber tribe founded the city of Salé on the right bank of the river mouth, and built a *ribat* (fortified camp) on a bluff at the western extremity of the estuary's south bank.

The Almohad sultan, Abd el Moumen, made the fortress his base for raids into Andalusia and called it Ribat el Fath (Ribat of Victory). His son, Yacoub el Mansour, began to build an

A Moroccan Glossary

Here is a selection of common Arabic and Berber words you are likely to encounter:

aïd	holy day	*makhzen*	storehouse, government
aïn	spring		
bâb	gate	*méchouar*	palace courtyard, reception area
baraka	divine blessing		
borj	fort	*medersa*	religious school
djébel	mountain	*medina*	old town
fondouk	warehouse, caravanserai	*mellah*	Jewish quarter
		moulay	master
jellaba	long-sleeved tunic	*moussem*	pilgrimage and festivities
jemaa	mosque		
kasbah	fortified part of Medina	*oued*	seasonal watercourse
kissaria	covered market	*ribat*	fortified military camp
ksar	fortified village		
(pl. ksour)		*souk*	market (streets)

A Rabati gent, prayer-mat beneath his arm, hurries through the Royal Palace Gardens.

Imperial City here in the 12th century AD, but when he died, the place became a backwater while Fès, Meknès and Marrakech prospered.

With the establishment of the Franco-Spanish Protectorate in 1912, Marshal Lyautey made Rabat the administrative capital, and when Morocco regained its full independence in 1956 the city became capital of the new kingdom.

MODERN RABAT

Rabat has many attractive public buildings, open squares and tree-lined boulevards, and is also characterized by a pleasant, relaxed atmosphere. **Avenue Mohammed V**, the main artery of modern Rabat, cuts a wide and sunny swath through the town, down past government buildings, banks, the railway station and the main post

office. Pedestrians throng the shady shopping arcades on either side, a pleasant place to stroll and browse, or to sip mint tea and plan your day's sightseeing.

THE MEDINA

If you follow Avenue Mohammed V northwards (turn left coming out of the railway station), you soon reach the entrance to Rabat's Medina. Pass through the 17th-century Andalusian wall, with the tidy municipal market on the left, **35** and then turn right into Rue es-Souïka. Although some of the shops along this street sell leather and copper items unquestionably aimed at the tourist trade, most cater strictly for local needs. As the minaret of the Grand Mosque comes into view on the right, the street enters the roofed-over Souk es Sebat, where you'll discover that modern department stores really have nothing on Moroccan markets when it comes to sheer variety: exquisite gold jewellery, a brace of beef trotters, a kilo of dried chick peas (roasted or unroasted) and a pair of comfortable yellow *babouches* (leather slippers) – where else could you buy such an assortment of things under the same roof?

Where the Souk es Sebat emerges into bright sunlight, turn left into the Rue des Consuls, the Medina's main tourist street. Here you can browse in shops selling jewellery, carpets and antiques; some also have *caftans* and *jellabas*, and many of the shopkeepers are familiar

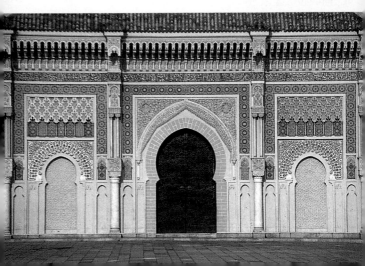

with the clothing sizes and requirements of foreign customers. The street has a pleasant community atmosphere, with shopkeepers sitting contentedly before their wares, waiting to be of service and watching the parade of passers-by.

At the end of Rue des Consuls you will see the massive and overpowering walls of the **Oudaïa Kasbah**. The impressive, monumental gate to this 12th-century fortress is one of the great architectural achievements of the Almohad dynasty. The kasbah occupies the site of the original *ribat* that gave the Moroccan capital its name – its hilltop position is obviously the best spot from which to defend the city. In the 18th century the sultan Moulay Ismaïl garrisoned a tribe of fierce Oudaïa Arabs in the kasbah for just that purpose.

Today the kasbah is a residential quarter. Pass through the gate (ignore any 'guides' who approach you – it is impossible to get lost here) into the narrow main street, Rue Jemaa, lined with iron-studded house doors set in picturesque

Rich decorations on the gates of Rabat's Royal Palace, and rich spices in the market.

doorways. At the far end is an open terrace overlooking the fortifications, with a fine view over the mouth of the Bou Regreg to Rabat's 'sister city', Salé. From here a short flight of steps leads down to a small restaurant and café overlooking the ocean.

For a restful break, return along Rue Jemaa and turn left down the Rue Bazzo to a pretty café, the Café Maure, where tables occupy a shady terrace beneath the spreading branches **37** of an ancient fig tree. A door from the terrace leads directly into the kasbah's delightful **Andalusian Garden**, planted with cypresses, lemon trees, datura, roses and bougainvillaea, and decorated with brass

A mounted warrior guards the entrance to the mausoleum of King Mohammed V.

cannons of 19th-century English and Spanish manufacture. A stairway climbs from the garden to a restored 17th-century palace which houses the city's **Museum of Moroccan Arts**. The collection includes blue and polychrome pottery, some very fine woodwork, and a lot of unusual gold and silver jewellery.

On the busy main road just downhill from the kasbah (Tarik el Marsa), you will find the **Musée National de l'Artisanat**, a small display of antique furniture, rugs and ceramics. The crafts co-operative opposite, the **Ensemble Artisanal**, sells the best modern work.

THE MAUSOLEUM OF MOHAMMED V

On the eastern edge of the new town lies a magnificent monument to the king who achieved independence for Morocco in 1956 (see p.22). Although it was built during the 1960s, the mausoleum is a clear celebration of traditional Moroccan craftsmanship. The tomb is resplendent with bright brass-work, cool marble, rich wood-work and polychrome ceramic tiles, and is one of the most lavish buildings in the world.

The entrance is flanked by guards dressed as Berber warriors, with billowing robes and antique flintlock rifles. Inside you will find yourself on a mezzanine balcony beneath a magnificent, carved wooden dome. On the floor below lies the onyx sarcophagus, a white island lost in a sea of polished black marble. A huge bronze lamp swings slowly over the tomb, suspended from a ceiling that glows darkly with rich gold ornamentation.

The mausoleum overlooks the venerable ruins of the Hassan Mosque, built by the Sultan Yacoub el Mansour at the end of the 12th century (Almohad dynasty). The sultan died before the mosque was completed, and the main structure fell victim to the elements; all that remains today are the parallel ranks of stumpy columns fringed by crumbling brick walls. The huge but unfinished minaret, now called the **Hassan Tower**, has survived un-scathed, and remains as a fine monument to Almohad architecture. The decoration on the higher panels resembles stylized layers of ascending clouds – an appropriately lofty and uplifting motif. The site, set high above the banks of the Bou Regreg, is superb, and the view from the terrace is particularly impressive.

ARCHAEOLOGICAL MUSEUM

To find Rabat's Archaeological Museum, simply head south on Avenue Mohammed V and pass to the left of the huge Sounna Mosque. Turn left on Rue Moulay Abd al Aziz the museum is first on your right. The collections cover Moroccan history from prehistoric times to the Muslim conquest, with the emphasis on the Phoenician and Roman eras.

The museum's showpiece is the Bronze Room, with fine bronze heads of King Juba II and Cato the Younger, a Roman statesman and philosopher. The other rooms contain marble sculptures, oil lamps, **39**

figurines, jewellery, coins and other finds from the archaeological sites at Sala Colonia, Lixus and Volubilis (see pp.10 and 52).

THE CHELLAH

The Roman town of Sala Colonia occupied a site that now lies outside the walls of Rabat. Long after the decline of the Eternal City, the Merinid sultans used the area as a cemetery for their own deads and, in the 14th century, built a strong defensive wall all around it. Known as the Chellah, the wall encloses lush, overgrown gardens littered saints' tombs and Roman ruins. To get there, walk past the Sounna Mosque on Avenue Yacoub el Mansour, and out through the city walls (see the map of Rabat on the cover of this guide).

The entrance leads through an imposing and ornate gateway, from which a long path leads downhill past overgrown Roman ruins to a little grove of bamboo and banana plants. On the right-hand side, behind a whitewashed tomb, is a stone basin full of crystal-clear water. In this quiet spot, childless women come and feed hard-boiled eggs to the slithery grey eels that inhabit the pond, in the hope that some ancient magic will one day bring them a son or daughter.

For a few dirhams, a young guide will show you around the ruined mosque next to the pond – its graceful minaret crowned with the untidy nests of migratory storks – and the neighbouring *medersa*, where traces of tilework on the arches and doorways testify to its former magnificence.

Doorways on either side of the *mihrab* (prayer niche) lead to a pretty garden and a tomb decorated with arabesques.

SALÉ

The Chellah looks out across the Bou Regreg to Rabat's sister city on the far bank of the river. Salé was founded in the 11th century and flourished as a trading centre in medieval times, reaching its height in the 14th century. Today, however, it is merely a suburb of Rabat. Its past glories are recalled by several impressive mosques and *medersas*, as well as the old defensive walls.

The bridge across the Bou Regreg below the Hassan Tower leads to the Bâb el Mrisa, the nearest of the main gates through the city walls. Enter the gate and wander through the *mellah*, or old Jewish quarter, to the souks that form the centre of the town. Chances

*S*torks have built their nests amid the overgrown ruins of the Chellah (left). A doorway (below).

41

The Pirates of Salé

In the 17th and 18th centuries the pirates of the Barbary Coast were a fearsome challenge to Christian supremacy of the seas. The fast and well-fitted Muslim privateers set out from points all along the Barbary Coast (the littoral of Tunisia, Algeria and Morocco), but the most celebrated corsairs in Atlantic waters were based in Rabat and Salé. These 'Sallée Rovers', as their English enemies called them, attacked not only Christian ships but also coastal towns in Spain, France and England. On at least one occasion Moroccan corsairs were seen operating in the waters off Newfoundland. Their last raid was in 1829.

are you won't see any other tourists – only local people frequent these busy and colourful markets.

From the souks, the Rue de la Grande Mosquée leads to Salé's **Grand Mosque**, with a tall and imposing stone doorway at the top of a flight of steps. Although you cannot enter the mosque unless you are a Muslim, you can visit its former religious college, the **Abou el Hassan Medersa**, across the way. Knock on the door to summon the *gardien* or janitor, who will show you around the deserted building. The walls are decorated with coloured ceramic tiles (called *zellij*), and above the tiles are carved cedar screens and delicate plasterwork, among the finest and most intricate in all Morocco.

The stairway leading to the roof passes two floors of tiny rooms for the theological students who once lived here. From the top of the stairs you can see into the courtyard of the mosque next door, and the panorama of Rabat, Salé and the river is superb.

You can return to Rabat by ferry. Just follow the crowds to the river below Bâb el Khebaz, where rowing boats await.

Casablanca

In 1515 the Portuguese built a small town on the Atlantic coast of Morocco and named it Casa Branca (meaning 'White House'). Spanish merchants settling here in the 18th century called it Casablanca, and it remained a backwater until it was occupied by the French in 1907. Under the Protectorate it grew to become Morocco's busiest port, its most populous city, and the economic and industrial capital of the kingdom, accounting for more than half of the country's industrial output. (In Arabic, the city is officially called Dar el Baida, – 'White House' – but most Moroccans refer to it as 'Casa'.)

The heart of modern Casablanca is **Place Mohammed V**, where all the thoroughfares converge beneath the towering

Brassware gleams in the sun in a quiet corner of Casablanca's Medina.

43

facade of the Hyatt Regency Hotel. At the turn of the century this was a patch of wasteland outside the Medina walls; today it is a bustling conglomeration of banks, hotels, restaurants, shops and offices.

The **Old Medina** lies between Place Mohammed V and the port, but it is a mere shadow of its more colourful counterparts in Fès and Marrakech. The streets leading down to the harbour are lined with tourist shops and hustlers.

Nearby, **Place des Nations-Unies**, with its grandiose public buildings, is Casablanca's administrative centre. The central fountain and gardens are surrounded by the City Hall, the law courts, the French Consulate, the Cathédrale du Sacré Cœur and the main post office, all lovely examples of 1930s Art Deco architecture. The cathedral is in the process of being converted to a theatre.

Casablanca's most unforgettable sight is without doubt the **Grand Mosque of Hassan II**, built on a vast platform of reclaimed land to the west of the **44** port. It is the world's biggest mosque outside Mecca, with a prayer hall that can accommodate up to 25,000 faithful (for the sake of comparison, London's St Paul's Cathedral holds a mere 2,000 people).

The building costs of over £500 million were raised entirely by public subscription, with all Moroccans contributing according to their means. Its construction required some 300,000 tonnes of concrete and 65,000sq m (700,00sq ft) of marble cladding, and occupied 30,000 labourers, craftsmen, engineers and architects from its inception in 1980 to its inauguration in 1994.

The huge minaret towers over 210m (700ft) above the waves and is topped with a green laser beam pointing in the direction of Mecca. The mosque is the tallest building in Morocco and boasts the tallest minaret in the world, with a lift to carry visitors to the top.

The minaret of Casablanca's mosque of Hassan II is the tallest in the world.

Meknès

Meknès was founded in the 10th century by a Berber tribe called the Meknassa, but it was the Alaouite sultan Moulay Ismaïl who put the city on the map when he chose it as the site for his new capital in the late 17th century.

A great admirer of France's Louis XIV, the sultan set about building an imperial city to rival the Sun King's Palace of Versailles. Christian slaves and local tribesmen laboured for years to realize Ismaïl's grandiose plan, which comprised a complex of 24 royal palaces, with mosques, barracks and ornamental gardens, surrounded by four sets of massive defensive walls. Following the death of Moulay Ismaïl, the Imperial City fell into ruin, but the 20th century brought restoration and rejuvenation.

MODERN MEKNÈS

Most visitors stay in the Ville Nouvelle, where the majority of the comfortable hotels are concentrated. If you arrive by train, be sure to alight at the Abdelkader station – the first stop coming from Rabat or Tangier. It is closer to the city-centre hotels than the main railway station, which is a little further on.

One of the best panoramas of the city can be enjoyed at the four-star **Hôtel Transatlantique**. From its hilltop vantage point you can look across the Boufekrane valley to the walls, rooftops and minarets of ancient Meknès ranged along the heights.

THE IMPERIAL CITY

The Imperial City is so extensive that it can be rather tiring to explore it all on foot – allow for at least two to three hours of walking. If you don't want to walk, you can take a tour by bus, or engage a taxi driver to show you around the principal sights of the city.

From Avenue Hassan II, the main avenue of the new town, a bridge crosses the valley of the Oued Boufekrane and leads uphill to **Place el Hédim**, in the heart of the old city. The

square has recently been renovated, and now boasts fancy streetlamps, fountains, and a mock-Andalusian arcade full to the brim of handicraft stalls.

Dominating the southern end of the square is the massive, monumental gateway of **Bâb Mansour**, perhaps Moulay Ismaïl's most impressive legacy. The intricate ornamentation and richly coloured tiles evoke the wealth and splendour of old Meknès and its imperial court. To the right of the Bâb Mansour is a smaller gate in similar style, the **Bâb Jamaa en Nouar** – less imposing, but still very grand.

Massive walls enclose Sultan Moulay Ismaïl's Imperial City in Meknès.

Pass through the Bâb Mansour and you'll find yourself on the great expanse of Place Lalla Aouda; continue through a second gate, the Bâb el Filala, to another square. The small, domed building to your right is the **Koubbet el Khiyatîn**, where the great sultan once received foreign ambassadors. A stairway beneath the pavilion leads down to the **47** massive subterranean vaults, which are said to have been used as a prison for the European slaves who laboured on the construction of the Imperial City. Legend has it that the underground chambers ran for over 7km (4 miles), and that up to 40,000 slaves were incarcerated here each night.

On the far side of the square an archway leads to the triple-arched entrance of **Moulay Ismaïl's Tomb** on the left. The doorway to the tomb enclosure is magnificent, and like the rest of the tomb complex it was renovated during the reign of Mohammed V. Once through the door, you pass through several elegant courtyards. Grass mats at the threshold of the memorial mosque remind you to leave your shoes and proceed in stockinged feet; the tomb is a sacred place of pilgrimage and prayer, and while non-Muslims are allowed into the ante-chamber, they must not enter the sanctuary of the mosque proper.

From the ante-chamber you can peek into the memorial mosque, where Sultan Moulay Ismaïl's tomb rests beneath sumptuously decorated horseshoe arches, watched over by four ornate French grandfather clocks, a gift to the sultan from King Louis XIV in 1700.

On leaving the tomb, take a left turn and follow the road through the left-hand arch of the **Bâb er Rih** (Gate of the Winds) to emerge into a rather forbidding 800m (875yd) long corridor squeezed in between two mighty walls. On the other side of the wall to the right is the **Dar el Makhzen**, or Royal Palace (not open to visitors), where the monarch stays during his visits to Meknès.

At the far end turn right past the main entrance to the Royal Palace and continue through another gate to reach the **Dar el Ma**, also known as the **Héri es Souani**. This large, square, vaulted building, dating from the 17th century, served both as a granary and feed store for Moulay Ismaïl's vast stables, which housed 12,000 steeds. The roof of the building now supports a pleasant café-garden with a fine view of the city and the huge **Aguedal Basin**,

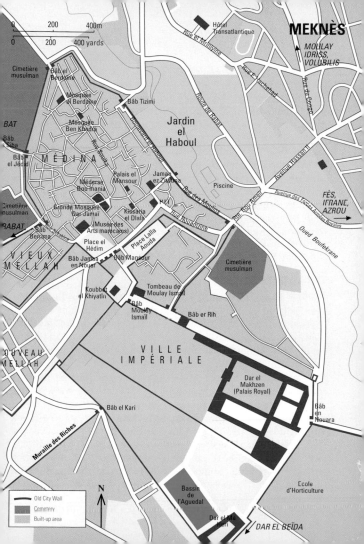

once used for the irrigation of the Imperial City's vast and luxuriant gardens.

The remains of Moulay Ismaïl's tremendous stables are attached to the granary. A short distance to the south proudly stands the **Dar el Beïda**, a thick-walled fortress of vaguely Eastern European aspect. Built as a sultan's palace in the late 18th century, it's been reconverted to serve as a military officers' training school.

THE MEDINA

Across Place el Hédim from the Bâb Mansour is an entrance gate into the Medina, and right beside it is the door of the **Dar Jamaï**, the century-old private palace of a minister of state, which houses Meknès's arts museum. The collections include wood carvings, silk embroidery, carpets from the Middle Atlas, tile-work, wrought-ironwork and jewellery. The reception room upstairs is fully – and somewhat eclectically – furnished. But the palace itself is perhaps the **50** major attraction. Bearing in mind that its fanciful architecture and intricate arabesque decoration were not intended for the sultan but merely for one of his ministers, you can imagine what splendours must lie within the Royal Palace.

A narrow alley to the right of the Dar Jamaï leads to the **Grand Mosque** with its elaborate entrances, ornate gates, green-tiled minaret and red-tiled roofs and cupolas. This is the largest and most sacred of the dozens of mosques in the city. It's also one of the oldest.

Across the street from the mosque is the **Bou Inania Medersa**. The *gardien* will give you a complete and fact-filled tour of this fine old religious college, built by Abu el Hassan in the 14th century. It's possible to climb to the roof for a bird's-eye view of the mosque and Medina.

The Meknès Medina is one of the tidiest in Morocco, and though many shops are in traditional style, others are strictly modern. As you explore the tortuous labyrinth of streets, you'll encounter the mingled scents of sweet incense, tangy citrus fruits, aromatic wood from the joiners' shops, and grilling meat from the numerous food stalls.

Glittering embroideries hang fluttering in the tiny windows of tiny shops, and men and boys chat while sewing away at *jellabas* and caftans. Other shops are filled from floor to ceiling with bales of cloth and spools of silken thread in every shade imaginable.

Children fill cans with water from bubbling fountains decorated with coloured faïence, while bearded old men shuffle out of the Grand Mosque after noontime prayers, and put on their shoes. The entrance to the mosque is carefully protected from the outside world by a carved wooden screen. Nearby, mighty blue-painted doors mark the entrance to an ancient souk specializing in blankets and *jellabas*. This is the **Kissaria el Dlala**, always crowded (except on Fridays) with men watching the action as individual blankets and garments are sold at auction.

Along the **Rue du Souk en Nejjarîn**, a variety of modern shops break the solid ranks of traditional carpenters' shops from which the street takes its name. But here and there you can still find craftsmen working away with traditional tools at benches worn smooth from centuries of use.

*F*ragrant rose petals perfume the air in the Medina of Meknès – one of the tidiest in Morocco.

Excursions from Meknès

VOLUBILIS

About 30km (19 miles) north of Meknès lies Volubilis, the former capital of the Roman province of Mauritania Tingitana and now the site of the most extensive and impressive Roman ruins in Morocco. Hire a *grand taxi* (see p.127) in Meknès to take you to both Volubilis and Moulay Idriss or,

if you have your own transport, follow the road to Tangier for 15km (10 miles) then turn right on a minor road. Soon the ruins will come into view, set on a triangular plateau abutting the foothills of the Zerhoun massif.

Volubilis was a flourishing Roman city from the time of Christ until the end of the 3rd century, when the Romans began to withdraw, but it remained an outpost of Christian culture until the Arab conquest in the 7th century. As one of the most important cities in Mauretania Tingitana, it was a rich and prosperous place, and many vestiges of its days of glory survive. From the café and open-air 'museum' at the entrance, take the path across a bridge to the ruins. Small red arrows point out the route of the visitors' path.

After passing a number of olive-oil presses, you come to the **House of Orpheus**, a luxurious mansion containing mosaics of Orpheus, the Chariot of Amphitrite, and the Nine Dolphins. Beyond, a broad, paved street takes you past the

Mosaics adorn the villas of Volubilis beneath the hilltop town of Moulay Idriss (right).

Public Baths to the **Forum**, where the impressive remains of the **Capitol** and the **Basilica** dominate the site. Ahead lies the massive **Triumphal Arch**, raised in honour of the Emperor Caracalla, which marks the western end of the city's main street, Decumanus Maximus; ruts worn by cart wheels can still be seen in parts of the stone paving.

The villas lining this street contain many fine **mosaics**, and it was here in fact that archaeologists discovered the bronzes now displayed in Rabat's Archaeological Museum (see p.39).

MOULAY IDRISS

Under 3km (2 miles) from Volubilis, the holy town of Moulay Idriss tumbles down the slopes of its twin hills, Khiber and Tasga. In between the two peaks lies the tomb and shrine of Moulay Idriss I, the 8th-century founder of Morocco's first Arab dynasty.

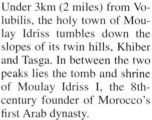

For much of the year the town is a sleepy backwater, but each September it is the focus for an annual *moussem* (holy festival), when thousands of pilgrims gather at the shrine of Morocco's first sultan. Both shrine and mosque are barred to non-Muslims, and visitors **53**

are not allowed to stay over-night in the town, but the set-ting is reason enough to visit.

The town's main square is lined with shops and stalls sel-ling religious artefacts, deco-rated candles and the locally produced nougat. The entrance to **Moulay Idriss's shrine** is at the far end of the square. Here, a wooden bar across the pas-sage reiterates the following warning: *L'accès n'est pas per-mis aux non-Musulmans* ('No entry to non-Muslims'). How-ever, one of the many unoffi-cial guides in the square will lead you through the narrow, winding alleyways of the Khi-ber to the famous viewpoint of the **Terrace of Sidi Abdallah el Hajjam**.

INTO THE MIDDLE ATLAS

In the cedar forests of the Middle Atlas lie the cooler hill towns of Azrou and Ifrane. **Azrou**, 60km (38 miles) south of Meknès, is built on a hill-side in the forest, next to the outcrop of rock (*azrou* in the Berber language) that gives the

town its name. It is famous not only for its peace and quiet, but also for its carpet weaving. The Berber tribe known as the Beni M'Guild set their looms in a central handicrafts market, and you can watch rugs being made as you shop for the fin-ished product. The Berber vil-lage of mud-brick houses with flat white roofs can be seen on the hillside above the town.

The road north from Azrou towards Ifrane provides spec-tacular views of the serried mountain ranges of the Middle Atlas. The resort of **Ifrane** was created by the French in 1929 as a summer retreat and winter sports centre. The many hotels do a booming business on sum-mer weekends (best to reserve in advance if you intend stay-ing overnight) when city folk escape to enjoy the cool, fra-grant mountain breezes. The surrounding cedar forests pro-vide pleasant, shady walks, often carpeted with wildflow-ers in spring. In winter, the ski area of **Mischliffen** (about 20 minutes' drive from Ifrane) provides very basic skiing fa-cilities from January to March.

The slopes are of interest only to beginners, but the scenery is truly enchanting.

Fès

Fès, the oldest and possibly greatest of Morocco's four Imperial Cities, is really three cities in one. Fès el Bali (Old Fès) was founded by Moulay Idriss II at the end of the 8th century, down in the valley of the Oued Fès. Five hundred years later, the Merinid sultans added many jewels of Hispano-Moorish architecture to the old city and built a new one, called Fès el Jédid (New Fès), outside the walls. Then, during the 20th century, the French built a modern city, the Ville Nouvelle, on the higher ground above the valley.

VILLE NOUVELLE

Most visitors arrive first in the Ville Nouvelle, where the railway station, bus station, tourist office and most of the hotels are concentrated. There is little to see here, but it's a good spot to get your bearings, plan your exploration of Fès el Bali, and perhaps hire a guide through your hotel or the tourist office.

The broad boulevard of Avenue Hassan II is the main axis of the modern town, but the

A jellaba-clad tour guide describes the courtyard of the Bou Inania Medersa.

most interesting cafés, restaurants and shops are to be found along **Avenue Mohammed V**. This tree-lined avenue is at its liveliest in the early evening, when the whole town turns out for a promenade.

FÈS EL JÉDID

From the tourist office on the Place de la Résistance, Boulevard Moulay Youssef leads to the wide open space of **Place du Commerce**, the gateway to Fès el Jédid. In the far right corner of the square a small gate marks the way into the crowded streets of the *mellah*, the old Jewish quarter. Take a stroll down the **Grande Rue du Mellah**, lined with shops selling household goods and food, and crammed with people, donkeys, trucks and mopeds. At the far end, cross the main street then pass through the massive **Bâb Semmarîn** into the bustle of the **Grande Rue de Fès el Jédid**, past piles of dates, figs and prickly pears, boxes of juicy watermelons and kebabs spluttering over makeshift grills.

At the end of the street, an archway on the left leads into a high-walled enclosure. Turn right through a gate for the Avenue des Français, which leads to the Bâb Boujeloud and Fès el Bali, but if you're feeling energetic and fancy a panoramic view of the old city, continue through a triple-arched gate into the **Vieux Méchouar**, a large courtyard, and then out through the Bâb Segma. From here, follow the left-hand side of the massive **Kasbah des Cherarda**, built in 1670 by Sultan Moulay Rachid to harbour his unruly Berber warriors, and turn right at the top of the hill. A walk of about 15 minutes along the main road leads to the **Borj Nord** (North Fort). This 16th-century fortress now houses an outstanding collection of arms from a 12-tonne cannon to a nine-barrelled pistol. From here there is a fine view across the rooftops of Fès el Bali, crammed into the valley below, with the roof of the Karaouine Mosque prominent in the centre. (If you don't want to walk, drive or take a taxi – see p.128.)

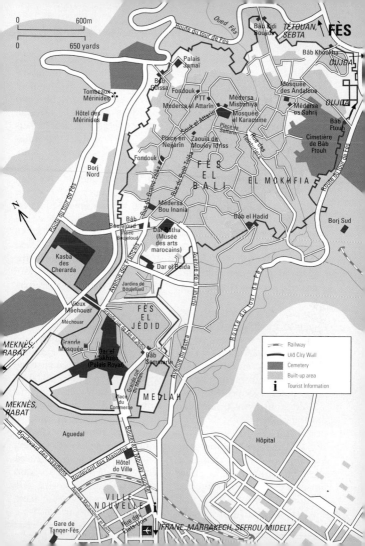

FÈS EL BALI

The Old City of Fès, or Fès el Bali, is one of Morocco's major attractions. It is a unique legacy from the past, a living medieval city that has survived almost intact, and is now listed as a World Heritage Site. Many of the inhabitants lead a way of life that has changed little since the 14th century, when the city was the religious, commercial and intellectual capital of Morocco.

Before plunging into the maze of streets and alleyways it's best to employ a guide, as it's all too easy to become lost. Licensed guides can be hired from the tourist offices found on Place Mohammed V in the Ville Nouvelle and at the Bâb Boujeloud, or from any of the larger hotels (see p.118).

Start from Place Boujeloud, the square that lies at the junction of Fès el Bali and Fès el Jédid. The monumental gate leading into the old Medina is the **Bâb Boujeloud**, a grand horseshoe arch flanked by two keyhole doorways. Two narrow streets lead from the gate

into the depths of the Medina – the Talâa Seghira (in front of you) and the Talâa Kebira (off slightly to your left, through an arch marked 'Kissariat Serajine'). Follow the Talâa Kebira, and a few minutes' walk will bring you to the Bou Inania Medersa, standing on your right-hand side.

The **Bou Inania Medersa**, built in the 1350s, is one of the glories of Hispano-Moorish architecture. As you leave the crowded street and enter the quiet courtyard you will find yourself bewitched by the serenity of the place. Polychrome tiles and a band of Kufic script adorn the lower walls, while above, the dark patina of aged stucco blends in harmoniously with the weathered cedarwood screens. The *muqarnas* (stalactite work) above the windows is particularly fine.

If the demands of restoration work allow, you may be allowed to go upstairs. Here you can see the tiny rooms where the theological students once lived; the little slot next to each door was not for mail, but for the students' daily ra-

58

tion of flat bread. There is also a grand view of the city from the rooftop.

As you leave the Medersa and return to the busy street, look up to the left at the curious **water-clock**, a strange and beautiful contraption of metal bowls and finely carved wood that exudes an air of mystery. Though its purpose was undoubtedly to establish the correct times for prayer, its maker and its method of operation have unfortunately been lost in the mists of time.

The street life of Fès el Bali provides endless fascination. Here you can watch a shirt-maker at work with his needle and thread, or a wood-turner with a small, bow-driven lathe. Even the children have an entrepreneurial spirit – you'll come across many tiny stands run by junior merchants.

The ornate arch of Bâb Bouje loud leads into the labyrinth of Fès el Bali – the Old City of Fès.

Your guide may point out one of the old **fondouks** along the way. These courtyards lined with small rooms once provided accommodation for travelling merchants, but are now used as workshops and storehouses by local craftsmen and guilds.

Continuing along the Talâa Kebira, at the foot of a hill, you will find the **Souk el Attarîn** (the perfumers', or spice merchants', market). Pause at leisure here to look over the shops full of pharmaceutical, cosmetic and herbal goods – tree bark and incense, twigs, roots, charms and potions are all on sale. Among the traditional druggists' shops are some specializing in souvenirs and Moroccan crafts. A few are set up in beautiful old mansions, and a shopping expedition here gives you the bonus of a tour through a traditional Moroccan house.

If you look down the first sidestreet to the right after you enter the souk, you will see a minaret covered in white plaster and green faience towering above an ornate gateway; this

is the **Zaouïa of Moulay Idriss II**, the founder of Fès and son of the first Moroccan Arab sovereign. You can pass the wooden bar which marks the limit of the sanctuary, and peer up the steps to the magnificent doors of the prayer room and the glittering chandeliers beyond. But entry is forbidden to non-Muslims, and you should also refrain from taking photographs. The *zaouïa* (monastery) dates back to the 9th century, but was rebuilt in the 13th and 18th centuries.

At the end of the Souk el Attarîn you approach the richest concentration of beautiful buildings in all of Fès. Centred on the Karaouine Mosque, this is one of the very oldest parts of the city, its foundation dating back a thousand years or more. The greatest architectural jewel is undoubtedly the **Karaouine Mosque**. Built during the late 9th century on the orders of a woman from Kairouan (in Tunisia), the mosque has been enlarged and embellished over the centuries. Today it is the most impressive structure in Fès, capable of sheltering 20,000 worshippers, and dazzling in the richness and detail of its decoration.

The mosque is also the seat of the Karaouine University, one of the oldest universities in the world. From early times Fès has been a centre of Islamic learning, and the Karaouine has been a focal point for both professors and students of religious law and theology. Although non-Muslims are not allowed to enter the mosque itself, the mosque's 14 gates allow an ample view of the ornate doorways and a glimpse of the vast interior.

Several interesting *medersas* line the streets around the Karaouine Mosque. The **Medersa El Attarîn** (dating from 1325), on the corner where the Souk El Attarîn meets the mosque, is smaller than its contemporary, the Bou Inania, but equally beautiful. From its roof there is a good view of the courtyard and minarets of the Karaouine Mosque.

Following the walls of the Karaouine clockwise from El Attarîn, you soon pass by the **Misbahiya Medersa** (built in

*S*tacks of half-cured hides await treatment in the vats of Fès's tanners' quarter.

1346). The building is now semi-derelict, but boasts a particularly pretty central fountain imported from Spain during the Saadian dynasty.

Continuing around the Karaouine walls you soon find **61**

yourself in the open space of **Place es Seffarîn**, the 'square of the brass- and copper-workers'. The banging of hammers on metal is incessant here, punctuated only by the squeal of red-hot metal being plunged into water to temper it. At the downhill end of the square, a small bridge crosses the Oued Fès. Just before it, through a gate on the right, is the **Rue des Teinturiers**, 'street of the dyers'. You can tell their shops from the dark stains along the street and the brightly coloured swaths of wool and cotton hanging out to dry.

For a terribly vivid look at medieval manufacturing methods, turn back sharp left from where you entered the square and head down towards another bridge. This is the **tanners' quarter**, where half-naked boy workers tread the skins in earthen vats filled with tanning chemicals or dyes, and stack the reeking hides on to donkeys for delivery to the leatherworkers' shops. The tanners' quarter is neither sweet-smelling nor uplifting; it is a true **62** slice of medieval life, where

the labourers risk dermatitis and lung disease for the paltry wage of a few dirhams a day.

The bridge by the tanners' quarter is known as the Bein El Moudoun (which translates as 'Between the Cities'), as it links the two oldest quarters of Fès. Cross the bridge into Fès el Andalous, the Andalusian quarter, and follow the main street (Rue Seftah) uphill until you reach a lofty portal at the top of a long flight of steps.

This marks the entrance of the **Andalusian Mosque**. You will notice that it is quite different from its counterparts across the river, although the materials used are the familiar tiles, wood and plaster. There is a special boldness, however, in the design which seems both foreign and exotic. The main door, built by an Almohad sultan in the early 1200s, is all there is to see for a great number of visitors, as entry is forbidden to non-Muslims.

Take the street to the right of the great door of the mosque to visit the **Medersa Es Sahrij**, dating from 1320. The building is well worth seeing for its very rich ceramic decoration and fine wood-carving.

Return to the Place Seffarîn. From here you can cross the bridge by the Rue des Teinturiers, turn right, and in a few minutes reach Place Er Rsif, where bus no. 19 will take you back to the Ville Nouvelle. Alternatively, continue to the far end of the Rue des Teinturiers and turn right into the covered passage of the Rue Cherratin, passing the Medersa es Cherratin, to reach the back of the Zaouïa of Moulay Idriss gateway (see p.60).

Here you will find the **women's entrance** to the sanctuary. The polychrome and gilt decoration of the façade is truly breathtaking, and this alone makes the stop worthwhile.

The copper plate below the window, covered with fancy wrought-iron work, once had a hole (now covered over) where women could insert an arm to 'capture' the saint's blessing, or *baraka* (see below). The saint lies at rest on the other side of the window.

Beyond the sanctuary is the **Place en Nejjarîn** (Square of the Joiners), the centre of Fès's cabinet- and furniture-making industry. The fountain built for the joiners is an exquisite, if somewhat well-worn, example of Moorish decorative art.

Baraka

The spiritual power called *baraka* has brought many a Moroccan sultan to the throne. Every Moroccan marabout (holy man) has been a possessor of *baraka*, and expectant pilgrims visit the tombs of these saints hoping to benefit from the blessing of their sanctity. Although not considered a saint, the King of Morocco has *baraka* by virtue of his function as a traditional ruler. In addition, the present king is a Sharif or descendant of the Prophet, a distinction shared by thousands of Moroccans, but which is all the more propitious when it applies to the ruler.

Follow the street to the right of the fountain, which passes beneath a building, then turn left and follow the main thoroughfare (Rue Zekak el Hajer, then Rue Souikat ben Safi, and finally Talâa Seghira) back to the Bâb Boujeloud (see p.58).

The **Museum of Moroccan Arts** is housed in a converted mansion, the **Dar Batha**, not far from Bâb Boujeloud. You cannot visit the Royal Palace in Fès, and so the palatial Dar Batha will give you some idea of how royalty lived a century ago, when the palace was built. The large garden is surrounded by arcades, and filled with cypresses, palms, jacaranda trees and spindly cacti 10m (33ft) high. The ceremonial chambers are now exhibition rooms in which you can scrutinize everything from medieval Arabic astrolabes to local carpets and costumes.

A DRIVE ROUND FÈS

A good way to get an idea of the city's layout is to drive along the **Route du Tour de Fès** (see the map on p.57), a simple 16km (10-mile) circuit that surrounds the two older parts of Fès and offers vast, commanding views from the heights to the north.

As it climbs past the walls of the Kasbah Cherarda, surrounded by cemeteries, the road soon passes the fortress of Borj Nord (see p.56). Further along is a viewpoint and the **Hôtel des Mérinides**. Stop for a moment, and try to pick out the landmarks of the city spread out in the valley below you, for when you are in the thick of the Medina it is impossible to appreciate the city's intricate layout. The ruined tombs of several Merinid sultans stand on a promontory to the east of the hotel.

Now the road winds down into the valley and through dense olive groves to touch at the Bâb Khoukha and Bâb Ftouh gates before skirting the city walls, passing the abandoned Borj Sud fortress – legend says that a tunnel beneath the city once linked it with Borj Nord – and returning to Place Mohammed V in the Ville Nouvelle (see p.55).

A Selection of
Hotels and Restaurants
in Morocco

Recommended Hotels

If you are visiting Morocco on a package tour, all your accommodation will have been arranged for you in advance. Our selection of hotels is therefore biased towards the independent traveller, concentrating on towns and cities that make useful 'base-camps' or stop-overs during a tour of the country.

As a basic guide we have used the symbols below to indicate prices for a double room with bath, including breakfast:

▊▊▊▊	over 500dh
▊▊▊	300-500dh
▊▊	150-300dh
▊	below 150dh

CASABLANCA

Foucauld ▊
52, rue Foucauld/Araibi Jilali
Tel. (02) 22.26.66
Basic hotel with few facilities, but cheap, clean, and centrally located. 21 rooms.

Hôtel de France ▊▊
2, rue Branly/Sharif Amzian
Tel. (02) 27.42.75/27.38.71
A friendly hotel offering pleasant rooms with ensuite bath and balcony overlooking pedestrian precinct. 37 rooms.

Guynemer ▊-▊▊
2, rue Pegoud
Tel. (02) 27.57.64/27.76.19
Clean and pleasant, with fading 1930s elegance, in quiet backstreet close to city centre. 28 rooms.

Hyatt Regency ▊▊▊▊
Place Mohammed V
Tel. (02) 26.12.34
Fax (02) 22.01.80
A five-star hotel providing luxury accommodation, including swimming pool, tennis courts and a night club. 229 rooms.

Moussafir ▊▊
Boulevard Ba Hamad
Tel. (02) 40.19.84
Bright, modern hotel situated next to the Casa-Voyageurs train station. 58 rooms.

ESSAOUIRA

Hôtel des Îles ▊▊▊
Boulevard Mohammed V
Tel. (04) 47.23.29; telex 710.42
Comfortable seafront hotel. Ask for a view over the bay. 75 rooms.

Sahara

Rue Oqba ibn Nafia
Tel. (04) 47.22.92
A basic hotel on Medina's main street, with large, quiet rooms set around a courtyard. 70 rooms.

Villa Maroc

10, rue Abdallah Ben Yassan
Tel. (04) 47.31.47
Beautiful, atmospheric hotel in a converted mansion, with rooms and suites arranged round a tiled courtyard. 22 rooms.

FÈS

Batha

Place Batha
Tel. (05) 63.64.37; telex 518.66M
Fine new hotel fronted by the former residence of the British Consul. Next to the Medina and Dar Batha museum. 61 rooms.

CTM

Boulevard Mohammed V
Tel. (05) 62.28.11
Old-fashioned, good-value hotel in the Ville Nouvelle. Next to the bus station. 25 rooms.

Mounia

60, rue Asilah
Tel. (05) 62.48.38; telex 518.01
Friendly, modern hotel with air-conditioned rooms. 94 rooms.

Palais Jamai

Bâb el Guissa, Medina
Tel. (05) 63.43.31
Fax (02) 63.50.96
One of Morocco's top hotels, set in a 19th-century vizier's palace, with panoramic views over the sprawling medina. A swimming pool and gardens complement the grand Moorish architecture and decor. 136 rooms.

MARRAKECH

Agdal

1, boulevard Zerktouni, Guéliz
Tel. (04) 43.36.70; telex 720.88
Attractive modern hotel in centre of Ville Nouvelle, with air-conditioning, swimming pool and private parking. 130 rooms.

CTM

Place Jemaa el Fna
Tel. (04) 44.23.35
Good cheap hotel, popular with independent travellers. Roof terrace provides prime views of the Jemaa el Fna. 33 rooms.

Gallia

30, rue de la Recette, Medina
Tel. (04) 44.59.13
One of the best-value hotels in the Medina, with quiet, spacious rooms around two attractive tiled courtyards. 19 rooms.

67

Grand Hôtel Tazi   ▌▌

*Corner of avenue el Mouahidine
and rue Bâb Agnaou*
Tel. (04) 44.24.52; telex 740.21
A large, old-fashioned place with
spacious rooms, bar and restaurant,
and a swimming pool. Good
value. 61 rooms.

Mamounia   ▌▌▌▌+

*Avenue Bâb Jdid
(edge of Medina)*
Tel. (04) 44.89.81
Fax (04) 44.46.60
One of the most expensive hotels
in Morocco, a luxurious palace
set in beautiful gardens, once the
favourite holiday retreat of Winston
Churchill. 232 rooms.

MEKNÈS

Majestic   ▌-▌▌

19, avenue Mohammed V
Tel. (05) 52.20.35
Friendly hotel, close to the Abdelkader
railway station. Spacious
rooms with balcony. 42 rooms.

Rif   ▌▌▌

Zankat Accra
Tel. (05) 52.25.91; telex 410.39
Bland but comfortable rooms, with
air-conditioning, TV and mini-bar.
Swimming pool, restaurant and
shop selling souvenirs, film, postcards,
stamps. 120 rooms.

Transatlantique   ▌▌▌▌

Rue el Meiniyine
Tel. (05) 52.50.50
Fax (05) 52.00.57
The best hotel in town, set high on
a hill with a grand view over the
Medina. Two restaurants and two
swimming pools. 121 rooms.

OUARZAZATE

Azghor   ▌▌▌

Boulevard Prince Moulay Rachid
Tel. (04) 88.26.12
Fax (04) 88.24.13
Four-star hotel with restaurant, bar
and swimming pool. Some rooms
have good views of the mountains
to the south. 109 rooms.

Es Saada   ▌

12, rue de la Poste. No telephone.
Good-value one-star hotel offering
clean, comfortable rooms with ensuite
bathroom, near to centre of
town. 26 rooms.

RABAT

Balima   ▌▌

Boulevard Mohammed V
Tel. (07) 70.77.55
Fax (07) 70.74.50
Old-fashioned pile with an atmosphere
of fading grandeur. Rooms
are large and reasonably comfortable,
and the hotel is conveniently

situated across the street from the railway station. 71 rooms.

Central   ▮

2, rue Al Basra
Tel. (07) 76.73.56

Next door to the Balima, and better value, with bright, spotlessly clean rooms. Ensuite bathroom costs extra. 34 rooms.

Safir   ▮▮▮▮+

Place Sidi Makhlouf
Tel. (07) 73.47.47
Fax (07) 72.21.55

Magnificent five-star palace on the bank of the Bou Regreg, with panoramic views of Salé, the Kasbah and the river. 197 rooms.

TANGIER

Africa   ▮▮-▮▮▮

17, avenue Moussa Ibn Noussair
Tel. (09) 93.55.11; telex 336.47

A comfortable mid-range hotel with a rooftop swimming pool, situated in the heart of the Ville Nouvelle. 86 rooms.

Continental   ▮▮

36, rue Dar El Baroud
Tel. (09) 93.10.24

Stylish old hotel deep inside the Medina, founded in 1888. Some rooms have good views over the bay. 57 rooms.

El Minzah   ▮▮▮▮

85, rue de la Liberté
Tel. (09) 93.58.85
Fax (09) 93.45.46

Tangier's top hotel, a five-star establishment built 50 years ago by the Marquis of Bute, set amid lush gardens with fine views over the bay. Two restaurants, swimming pool, tennis court. 100 rooms.

TAROUDANNT

Gazelle d'Or   ▮▮▮▮+

P32, 2km (1 mile) west of town
Tel. (08) 85.20.39
Fax (08) 85.25.37

A famous (and very expensive) hotel, set in a converted hunting lodge built by a French Baron in the 1920s and a popular winter retreat. Guests stay in bungalows in the extensive gardens, and can enjoy tennis, horse riding and falconry. 23 rooms.

ZAGORA

La Fibule   ▮▮

500m (550yd) on road to M'Hamid
Tel. (04) 84.73.18

Just out of Zagora, this hotel is full of character – it's modelled on a Berber *ksar*, with a palm-fringed garden and swimming pool, and with camels tethered in the parking lot. 40 rooms.

69

Recommended Restaurants

Restaurants offering Moroccan dishes such as couscous, *tajines* and *brochettes* are ten-a-penny in the main tourist spots, and there is little to choose between them apart from price; generally, the further away from the beach, main square or main avenue, the cheaper. You can eat well for very little money if you wander off the beaten track, especially in the Medina.

Below is a list of restaurants recommended by Berlitz. We have concentrated on the better-quality Moroccan restaurants and those offering alternatives to local cuisine – you may tire of couscous and *brochettes* if you stay in the country for more than a week! If you find other places worth recommending we'd be pleased to hear from you.

As a basic guide we have used the following symbols in order to give some idea of the price of a three-course meal for two, excluding drinks:

▐▐▐	over 300dh
▐▐	150-300dh
▐	below 150dh

AGADIR

Madame Marquez ▐▐-▐▐▐
86, rue des Oranges
Tel. 84.10.72
An intimate seafood restaurant offering specialities from the Caribbean island of Martinique.

Mille et Une Nuits ▐
Place Lahcen Tamri
No phone
Cheap and lively Moroccan restaurant off Avenue 29 Février at the back of town, where you can fill up with kebabs, couscous, etc.

Miramar ▐▐
Hôtel Miramar
Boulevard Mohammed V
Tel. 84.07.70
Stylish restaurant overlooking the beach and close to the fishing harbour, serving fine seafood and Italian dishes.

Phi Long ▐-▐▐
Avenue Hassan II
Tel. 84.21.08
This attractive Vietnamese restaurant provides a change from Moroccan specialities, and represents good value for money.

CASABLANCA

A Ma Bretagne ||||+
Boulevard de la Corniche
Sidi Abderrahman
Tel. 36.21.12
Gourmet French restaurant over-looking the sea, 10km (6 miles) west of city centre. Probably Morocco's top restaurant, with superb seafood. Closed Sunday, August.

Etoile Marocaine |
107, rue Allal Ben Abdallah
No phone
A friendly and inexpensive restaurant offering traditional Moroccan dishes, although the décor is rather over the top

Natraj ||–|||
13, rue Chenier
Tel. 29.56.50
Small and friendly Indian restaurant with English-speaking owner, serving delicious bhaji, pakora, naan, and a wide range of traditional curries.

Port de Pêche ||–|||
Le Port de Pêche
Tel. 31.85.61
Excellent seafood restaurant located right beside the fishing harbour. Apart from fresh fish, shellfish and lobster, one of the house specialities is paella.

ESSAOUIRA

Café Essalam |
Place Prince Moulay el Hassan
No phone
Excellent fish, *tajines* and couscous in this pleasant little restaurant on the attractive town square.

Chez Sam |–||
Port de Pêche. No phone.
A well-known seafood restaurant out at the end of the quay past the boatbuilders' yards, that looks like a boathouse. Lively atmosphere and excellent food.

FÈS

El Ambra ||||
47, route d'Immouzer
Tel. 64.16.87
Generally regarded as the city's top restaurant, offering Moroccan banquets and other specialities. Call in advance to reserve a table and discuss the menu.

Dar Saada ||–|||
21, Souk Attarine, Medina
Tel. 63.33.43
A sumptuously decorated palace in the heart of Old Fès, offering traditional Moroccan banquets. *Méchoui* (spit-roast whole lamb) available with one day's notice. Popular with tour groups.

71

MARRAKECH

Foucauld   ‖
Av. el Mouahidine. Tel. 44.54.99
Palatial décor and Moroccan specialities, including *bstilla*, at bargain prices. Good place to splurge without breaking the bank.

Yacout   ‖‖+
*79, Sidi Ahmed Soussi, Medina
Tel. 31.01.04*
Sumptuous mansion in the heart of the Medina, offering Moroccan and French gourmet cuisine in an Andalusian courtyard. Advance reservations essential.

MEKNÈS

Hôtel   ‖-‖‖
Transatlantique
*Rue el Meiniyine, Ville Nouvelle
Tel. 52.00.02*
Set in Meknès's only five-star hotel, it serves excellent Moroccan and European cuisine. Try to get there around dusk for a fine view of the old town.

Zitouna   ‖
*44, Jamaa Zitouna, Medina
Tel. 53.02.81*
Probably the best traditional Moroccan restaurant in the Medina, with a splendid décor and some fine food.

OUARZAZATE

Chez Dimitri   ‖
Av. Mohammed V. Tel. 88.26.53
A local institution, run by an ex-legionnaire, and very popular. Good French and Moroccan food at reasonable prices.

RABAT

Diffa   ‖‖+
*Hôtel Tour Hassan
26, av. Abderrahman Anmegou
Tel. 72.14.01*
The capital's top restaurant for traditional Moroccan cuisine. Advance reservations essential.

Restaurant de la   ‖-‖
Plage
Plage des Oudaïas. Tel. 72.31.48
Good-value seafood restaurant, overlooking the beach below the Oudaïa Kasbah. Try to get a window seat and watch the sun set beyond the Atlantic surf.

TANGIER

El Korsan   ‖‖+
Hôtel El Minzah, 85, rue de la Liberté. Tel. 93.58.85
Tangier's best Moroccan restaurant will prepare *méchoui* (whole spit lamb) if ordered at least a day in advance.

Marrakech

The route south from Casablanca passes first through the rolling agricultural land of the Chaouia region, then enters a barren, rocky plain, where the red earth is torn by outcroppings of shattered black rock and tiny walled villages dot the landscape. Then suddenly, breasting a rise, you are confronted by what seems to be a mirage: a vast expanse of brilliant-green palm trees shimmering in the heat haze, and broken only by the pink walls of Marrakech, set against the breathtaking backdrop of the snow-capped peaks of the High Atlas.

For almost a thousand years Marrakech has been an imposing and dominant city. The fourth of Morocco's Imperial Cities, it was founded in 1062 by Yusuf ibn Tashfin, and acted as the capital of the kingdom under the Almoravid and Almohad dynasties until 1269, and then again under the Saadians in the 16th century.

Visiting Europeans mispronounced its name as 'Morocco', and thus the city gave its name to the kingdom.

Now Marrakech is the commercial centre for the High Atlas and the Moroccan Sahara, and a prime destination for European tourists in search of winter sun. The ancient Medina is flanked by the new town of Guéliz, a modern city of wide boulevards full of cars, trucks, buses, motorbikes, *calèches* and donkey-carts. Here you will find the more expensive cafés, hotels, shops and restaurants, car hire agencies, banks and airline offices. Most people, however, head along Avenue Mohammed V to the famous Jemaa el Fna.

JEMAA EL FNA

Near the eastern end of Avenue Mohammed V stands the city's most famous landmark, the 70m (230ft) high **Koutoubia Minaret**. The finest of the three great 12th-century Almohad minarets (the others are the Hassan Tower in Rabat and the Giralda in Seville), it established the classical proportions of subsequent minarets

73

in Morocco. Each face of the Koutoubia presents a different decorative pattern; today a few blue tiles testify to the former splendour of its decoration.

The street opposite the minaret leads into the wide open space of the Jemaa el Fna, which is probably the most famous city square in all North Africa. 'The Assembly of the Dead' is hardly an appropriate name for the liveliest square in Marrakech, but that is one possible translation of Jemaa el Fna. The name probably dates from the time of a particularly ruthless sultan, who displayed the heads of those who displeased him around the square.

Jemaa el Fna is the heart of traditional Marrakech. Arrive just before darkness falls, when the Koutoubia Minaret is silhouetted against a pink and crimson sky, and the crowds mill thicker than ever. You will see street entertainment at its best – bands of Berber musicians and dancers, troupes of acrobats, fire-eaters, sword-swallowers, snake-charmers, storytellers and boxers. Performers lead monkeys and liz-

ards past stalls selling orange juice, roasted chick peas, peanuts, hard-boiled eggs, sweet fritters, kebabs and *tajines* (see p.101). Around the edges of the square are the 'service industries' – scribes, travelling dentists with neat piles of pulled teeth, doctors with phials of evil-looking liquids, and grinning barbers stropping their cut-throat razors.

You'll soon feel like seeking refuge in one of the cafés bordering the square, some of which have rooftop terraces offering a grandstand view of the proceedings.

THE SOUKS

The souks, or markets, of the Medina occupy a maze of narrow streets to the north of Jemaa el Fna. They are at their busiest in the early morning and late afternoon, the most interesting times to visit. A guide is not really necessary, but will make things easier if your time is limited. Official guides can be hired from the tourist office or any of the larger hotels (see p.118).

74

The main entrance to the souks is at the opposite end of the square from the Koutoubia Minaret. The alley directly opposite the Café de France, and just left of the Restaurant al Fath, will take you through the potters' souk to the **Rue Souk Smarine** – the main thoroughfare, striped with sunshine and shadow, and lined with the most expensive crafts shops.

Where the street forks, take the right-hand branch. Immediately on the right, a narrow lane leads into a small square where you will find the **wool market** and the **apothecaries' souk**. Here, stallholders will

Brightly coloured skeins of wool dry in the sun in the dyers' souk of Marrakech.

demonstrate the spices, roots and herbs used in medicine, magic and cosmetics – mandrake root is used for aphrodisiacs; argan oil for massage; the mineral antimonite, finely ground, makes kohl to outline the eyes; and countless jars abound, filled with arcane objects for use in magic spells.

Back on the main street, Souk el Kebir, you soon reach **75** the **Kissarias** (covered markets) in the heart of the souk, where the stalls sell a variety of goods. Further on, follow your nose to the luxurious smells of the **Souk Cherratîn** (leather market), where shops are packed with jackets, bags, purses, sandals and boots.

Head leftwards through the leather souk, then turn right to reach a small open space with a domed shrine on the right. This is the 11th-century **Koubba Ba'adiyn**, the only surviving Almoravid building in the city. The next street on the right leads along the wall of the Ben Youssef Mosque; turn left at the far end to find the inconspicuous entrance to the Medersa Ben Youssef.

The **Medersa Ben Youssef** was founded in the 14th century, but was rebuilt in Andalusian style by the Saadians in the 16th century. It is the largest *medersa* in Morocco, and the courtyard is bordered on two sides by delicate arcades, reminiscent of the Alhambra Palace in Granada.

On your return trip to the Jemaa el Fna, keep to the right of the Kissarias, through the **Souk des Bâbouches** (slipper market). Off to the right, use your nose again to track down the **Souk Chouari** (carpenters' souk), where the heady scent of sandalwood and cedar perfumes the air. Turning left along Rue Souk Attarîn, you soon pass the **Souk des Teinturiers**, or dyers' souk, hung with brightly coloured skeins of freshly dyed wool. Rue Souk Attarîn then merges with Souk Smarine, which leads back to the Jemaa el Fna (see p.73).

THE MEDINA

The part of the Medina that lies to the south of Jemaa el Fna contains a number of splendid monuments to the dynasties that once ruled Morocco. Follow the Rue du Bâb Aguenaou south from Jemaa el Fna until you reach Bâb er Rob, a huge gate in the city wall. Go left through another gate, the Bâb Aguenaou, and you will see the Mosque el Mansour ahead. To its right is the narrow entrance to the delightful Saadian Tombs.

The **Saadian Tombs**, built by Ahmed el Mansour in the 16th century, were walled up around a hundred years later by the vengeful Sultan Moulay Ismaïl. They lay forgotten until 1917, when the French cut a passageway through the wall to allow tourists to admire the rooms where the Saadian imperial families lie buried. Most impressive is the Room of the Twelve Columns, where the tombs of Ahmed el Mansour, his son and his grandson are marked by marble slabs.

Retrace your steps towards the Jemaa el Fna as far as the Grand Hôtel Tazi, then turn right along Avenue Houmman el Fetouaki to the square called Place des Ferblantiers. Walk through a gate on the right into a high-walled enclosure; a ramp on the right leads up to the palace of **El Badi**. This was once the sumptuous residence of Ahmed el Mansour, but it was systematically stripped of its wealth and largely destroyed by the jealous Moulay Ismaïl. Today, you will have to use your imagination to picture the opulence of the original, but the sheer scale of the place is still impressive.

Return to Place des Ferblantiers and bear right; a few minutes' walk will bring you to the **Bahia Palace**. This was the residence of the Chief Vizier

This graceful fountain adorns a courtyard in the Medina's elegant Bahia Palace.

to Sultan Moulay el Hassan, built during the final years of the 19th century. A guide will lead you through luxurious apartments to the harem, a beautiful courtyard with separate chambers for the Vizier's four wives. A small forest of palms, cypress and ivy in the centre of the court is watered by gurgling fountains, and provided with a shady gazebo. The favourite of the four had a sumptuous apartment secluded from the others.

From the Bahia it's a short but many-cornered way to the **Dar Si Saïd**, another palace built by the same family as the Bahia, and now the home of Marrakech's Museum of Moroccan Arts. The palace rooms are grandiose indeed, especially the magnificent reception room upstairs. The exhibition rooms are arranged around a delightful Andalusian courtyard, with displays of robes, weapons, metalwork and jewellery. A pictorial display outlines the major architectural monuments of each Moroccan dynasty from the Idrissids to the Alaouites.

AGUEDAL AND MÉNARA GARDENS

South of the Medina and the modern Royal Palace lies the **Aguedal Garden**, a vast royal pleasure garden almost 3km (2 miles) long. Water sparkles through the irrigation ditches, between the groves of orange, lemon, fig and pomegranate trees. In the heart of the gardens lies a series of huge irrigation pools, whose water has been brought from the foot of the Atlas Mountains by a system of canals. Fruit trees and flowers provide welcome shade for a quiet stroll or a picnic. (The gardens are closed when the king is in residence, usually during the winter months.)

The **Ménara** is an extensive olive grove to the west of the city. At its centre an enormous pool reflects the blue of the sky, and at one end a pavilion provides a vantage point for gazing at the gardens and the snow-capped mountains. The pool and gardens date from the time of the Almohads – but succeeding rulers have maintained and improved them.

West to the Atlantic Coast

Marrakech is the starting point for trips throughout southern Morocco. The most popular destinations are Essaouira and Agadir on the Atlantic coast, and Ouarzazate on the far side of the Atlas Mountains.

The most dramatic route to the Atlantic coast crosses the Atlas Mountains through the **Tizi n'Test** pass, which reaches a height of 2,092m (6,860ft) above sea level. The route then leads through the village of **Asni**, which has a lively week- end market and is where a side road leads off to Imlil, the base for climbing **Djébel Toubkal**, at 4,167m (13,670ft) the high- est peak in the Atlas.

Beyond Asni the road is narrow and twisting, and the scenery becomes increasingly impressive as you climb into bare, rocky hills of red and ochre earth, interspersed with shattered crags of dark brown rock. Above the village of Idni

*T**he golden sands of Agadir attract sun-seeking tourists from all over Europe.*

79

there is a fine view back down the valley, with Toubkal towering high in the background. At the summit of the pass there is a small restaurant, where you can enjoy a panorama southwards across the Souss Valley, with the ridge of the Anti-Atlas Mountains rising majestically above the haze.

The road descends quickly to join Highway P32, where you turn right towards the town of Taroudannt.

TAROUDANNT

One single glimpse of Taroudannt, 225km (140 miles) from Marrakech, can tell you its whole history. Surrounded by olive groves, citrus orchards and green fields, it is at the centre of the rich Souss Valley, well watered with the melting snows of the High Atlas.

At a time when all coastal towns were open to naval attack, Taroudannt's inland location and high walls made it the natural and impregnable capital of the region. The gigantic fortifications, built by the Saadians during the 16th century,

have been kept in good repair, and provide the most striking attraction of the town to this day. Within the walls, the dusty squares and shady souks offer excellent shopping opportunities for carpets, leather goods and Berber jewellery.

AGADIR

Agadir lies 70km (43 miles) beyond Taroudannt, and offers a complete contrast to that ancient town. Although the name comes from a 16th-century *agadir* (fortress) on a hilltop to the north, the city itself is completely new. A terrible earthquake in 1960 levelled the old town, killing 15,000 people and leaving over 20,000 homeless. A new city, purpose-built as a holiday resort, was raised to replace it around the curve of golden sand that lines the impressive bay.

Bold, modern architecture, wide, tree-lined avenues, open squares and pedestrian precincts contrast markedly with the narrow, crowded streets of traditional Moroccan towns. The city centre revolves around the huge shopping centre of **Place du Prince Héritier Sidi Mohammed**.

A band of low-rise hotels separates the centre from Agadir's finest feature, its **beach**. This splendid swath of fine-grained sand stretches as far as the eye can see for 10km (6 miles) to the south, and is kept meticulously clean. However, this is the Atlantic coast – the ocean water is best reserved for strong swimmers.

As evening falls, the promenade comes into its own as a place for a pleasant beachside stroll before watching the sun set on the bay from one of the many sidewalk cafés.

EXCURSION FROM AGADIR

The mountains of the Anti-Atlas reach the coast south of Agadir, forming a natural barrier between the Souss and the Sahara. Much of the ancient caravan traffic made a detour to skirt the mountains by following the coastal route, bringing prosperity to the towns of Tiznit and Goulimine which lay along the way.

A good, two-lane highway leads south from Agadir across desolate, stony plains dotted here and there with patches of scrub and stunted trees. After about 90km (65 miles) you get

Tree-Climbing Goats

The country between Agadir and Essaouira is known as Le Pays de L'Arganier, or 'The Land of the Argan Tree'. The argan is a relative of the olive, a twisted, tortured-looking tree whose fruit is eaten by the local goats. The goats have become adept at climbing into its branches to graze, and the local goatherds will try to get you to stop and take photos of their arboreal flocks, then demand a fee of a few dirhams. Other boys will leap from the roadside in an attempt to sell bottles of argan oil, a pungent oil much used in Moroccan cuisine.

your first glimpse of palm trees and sand, before the pink walls of Tiznit heave into view.

Tiznit is a fortified desert oasis, protected by a massive, crenellated wall. Despite its ancient appearance, Tiznit was founded only a century ago by Sultan Moulay Hassan to help pacify the southern tribes. The town itself has little to offer the tourist, except the interesting little jewellers' souk, a good place to look for old Berber brooches and pins. The coast at Aglou-Plage, 17km (10 miles) west of town, boasts a magnificent surf beach.

A challenging and scenic four-hour drive inland from Tiznit leads in roughly 110km (68 miles) to the mountain village of **Tafraoute**. This relaxed backwater is surrounded by magnificent mountain scenery, and offers many possibilities for the keen walker and mountain-biker (bikes can be

Artist Jean Veran's Les Pierres Bleues (Painted Rocks) highlight the rugged beauty of Tafraoute.

hired in town). But Tafraoute is best known for **Les Pierres Bleues** (The Painted Rocks). In 1984 the Belgian artist Jean Veran covered entire rock outcrops in blue paint to create a giant 'work of art', giving a whole new meaning to the term 'landscape painting'.

Continuing south from Tiznit, you eventually reach **Goulimine**, 200km (124 miles) from Agadir and right at the very edge of the Sahara. The town was once famous for its Saturday **camel market**, but the arrival in the 1930s of motorized transport heralded the dawn of a new age and the end of a once thriving camel trade.

Today, the camels are few in number, and are there mainly to be photographed by coach parties from Agadir. However, the market deals in many other local goods, and can be quite interesting; another attraction is the famous 'Blue Men' of the desert, the Tuareg nomads whose skin takes on a blue colour from the indigo dye in their robes.

Apart from the colour and commotion of its market day,

Goulimine has a small collection of eating places, a few shops, and an old *ksar*, or fortress. The *moussem* (festival) of Sidi M'Hamed Benamar, in early June, attracts tribesmen from the desert.

ESSAOUIRA

The road north from Agadir passes through some fine scenery, with many remote and beautiful beaches, and white villages set amidst groves of argan trees (see p.81).

After roughly 173km (106 miles) you come to the fortified port of Essaouira 175km (109 miles) direct from Marrakech. This attractive town is just over 200 years old, built by Sultan Mohammed ibn Abdallah as a military port. The town plan was drawn up by a French architect who was a prisoner of the sultan, and so the streets are rather more orderly than the jumble of tortuous alleys normally found in a Moroccan Medina.

An attractive **beach** on the south side is served by a couple of hotels and restaurants, **83** and draws large numbers of European windsurfers. At the town end of the beach is the fishing and boatbuilding harbour, and the **skala** (gun battery), part of the old port's defences; from there you get a good view of the town walls.

Beside the *skala* is the Marine Gate, which leads past an inner harbour lined with fish stalls to the little **town square** called Place Prince Moulay el Hassan, where there is a good selection of attractive café-restaurants. Off to the right is the main street, lined with tidy shops and little souks, and where the whitewashed buildings are set off by blue-painted doors and shutters.

The souks are reputed for the **carpenters' workshops**, where craftsmen produce delicate marquetry work using the local *thuya* wood.

*D*ramatic fortifications guard the entrance to the harbour at Essaouira – once a military port.

South to the Sahara

The other major route across the High Atlas leads out of Marrakech and over the spectacular 2,260m (7,400ft) **Tizi n'Tichka** pass to the Drâa Valley and the town of Ouarzazate. This pass is longer than the Tizi n'Test, but it is easier to drive and the scenery is more impressive. You'll come across stalls at every bend selling **fossils and minerals**, and the more enterprising boys run out to your car offering amethysts, ammonites, geodes and other treasures. The Berber villages seem to grow out of the hollows in the hillsides, flat-roofed, low and angular, the same colour as the earth.

As you descend on the far side of the pass you feel the hot breath of the desert, and down in the valley the first *ksour* appear, fortified villages with pink mud walls, now crumbling in picturesque ruin. Finally, 204km (128 miles) out of Marrakech, you reach the desert town of **Ouarzazate**. A new town, Ouarzazate was built in 1928 as a garrison post on the threshold of the Sahara. Today it is best known as a desert resort and movie location; the films *Lawrence of Arabia* and *The Sheltering Sky* were shot nearby at Aït Benhaddou. The way east leads along the Dadès Valley to the spectacular Dadès and Todra gorges, while to the south lies the beautiful Drâa Valley, Zagora and, ultimately, the sands of the Sahara Desert.

THE DRÂA VALLEY

The highway south from Ouarzazate leads across barren and rocky plains before climbing over a pass and descending through spectacular stratified rock scenery to the village of **Agdz** – northern Drâa's administrative centre – with the peak of Djébel Kissane rising like a massive Bedouin tent in the background.

Here the road joins the **Drâa Valley**, a wide green swath of date palms and pink mud villages squeezed between great scarps of naked yellow rock. **85**

There are impressive *ksour* at Tamnougalt, Timiderte and Tinzoulin. The Drâa is Morocco's longest river, but it is only after very heavy rains that it manages to flow all the way from the slopes of the Atlas to its mouth on the Atlantic coast, near Tan Tan.

*W*alls of baked mud characterize the houses in the desert outpost of Ouarzazate.

The valley narrows to a rocky defile for a short way, then opens out before reaching the oasis town of **Zagora**, lying 164km (103 miles) away from Ouarzazate. There is little to see in Zagora, but it has a number of good hotels and is a jumping-off point for trips into the Sahara Desert and palmeries. Djébel Zagora, a black, volcanic mountain dominates the town. The tarmac road continues another 98km (61 miles) to M'Hamid, passing oases

and *ksour* along the way. You can arrange desert excursions by Land Rover or camel at any of the main hotels.

THE DADÈS VALLEY

A good road leads east from Ouarzazate along the broad Dadès Valley, with the slopes of the High Atlas on the left and the jagged desert peaks of the Anti-Atlas to the right. At Boumalne, turn left on a minor road which leads to the village of Msemrir. (If you do not have your own transport, buses or taxi rides are available from Msemrir.)

The road from the village passes through the fantastic scenery of the **Dadès Gorge**. The rock strata here are nearly vertical, and have been eroded into weird fins and razorback ridges of brick red, green and ochre. Beyond the splendid kasbah at Aït Arbi the river disappears into a narrow gorge, and the road switchbacks over a ridge to the spectacular upper valley. The valley floor is bright with almond and walnut trees and yellow-green fields

of maize spread beneath the little, picturesque villages of pink mud houses. After 25km (15 miles), the valley narrows to a gorge proper, and the tarmac road ends. (With a four-wheel-drive vehicle, it is, in fact, possible to continue into the mountains and descend the Todra Gorge.)

Beyond Boumalne the main road climbs on to a barren plateau, where the rocks have been burnished to an iridescent bronze by the relentless sun, before descending to the administrative centre of **Tinerhir**, well equipped with hotels and restaurants.

A minor road on the far side of town leads left through a luxuriant **palmery**, and after some 15km (9 miles) reaches the mouth of the **Todra Gorge**, a popular destination for travellers. This truly magnificent limestone ravine is far more impressive than that at Dadès, being 300m (985ft) deep but just 10m (32ft) wide at its narrowest point. If you want to spend the night here, there are a few simple hotels and campsites at the head of the palmery. **87**

What to Do

Shopping

The souks of Morocco are one of the country's greatest attractions. Exploring these labyrinths of narrow streets and alleyways lined with exotic goods can make you feel like a character out of *The Arabian Nights*. Every town and village has its souk, no matter how small: cities such as Fès and Marrakech have entire districts crammed with souks, each one dedicated to a particular trade, while country villages have a weekly general market. Some of the more interesting weekly souks are listed below:

Agadir	Sunday
Ifrane	Sunday
Moulay Idriss	Saturday
Ouarzazate	Sunday
Tafraoute	Wednesday
Taroudannt	Thursday and Sunday
Tinerhir	Monday
Zagora	Wednesday and Sunday

Bargaining

In an economy where many products are handmade, each item has a different value depending on the quality of the workmanship. Thus, bargaining is a way of determining the proper price, and not simply a way for a shopkeeper to obtain more money from one customer than from the next. To secure the best price, however, you must get to know the market by browsing in several shops and asking the prices of comparable pieces.

When you find something you want to buy, ask the shopkeeper how much it costs, and then offer around half of what you're prepared to pay. The owner will feign amazement at such an insultingly low price and discourse at length on the quality of the workmanship, but will eventually suggest a lower price. You, of course, will plead poverty and suggest that you can obtain the same thing more cheaply elsewhere, but end up making an offer slightly higher than your first. Ideally, you should have a partner who feigns impatience and tries to get you to leave. This good-natured banter will continue back and forth until you settle on a mutually acceptable price. If the item is expensive, say a carpet, a leather jacket or a silver teapot, the process might involve several glasses of mint tea and a good half-hour of your time.

Two golden rules are: never to begin bargaining for something you do not genuinely intend to buy, and never to offer a price that you are not prepared to pay.

If you prefer not to bargain, visit the local Ensemble Artisanal, a state-run crafts shop that has fixed prices (ask at the tourist office for the nearest one). Here you can gain some idea of the range of crafts available and the prices you can expect to pay. (The variety will be greater and the prices a little lower in the souks.)

Bargaining for carpets is thirsty work – glasses of mint tea ease the proceedings.

What to Buy

Carpets and Rugs: Moroccan carpets generally have a deeper pile and a looser weave of larger knots than the more familiar Persian or Turkish ones. The finest and most expensive are those from Rabat; Marrakech and Meknès are also good places to buy. Also very attractive are the small woven rugs called *killims*, which are made mostly in the villages of the Middle Atlas; the carpet

M eknès craftsmen produce some of Morocco's finest pottery and ceramics.

souk in Azrou comes highly recommended.

Jewellery: chunky Berber jewellery made of silver, amber and semi-precious stones is strikingly beautiful, and can be found at a fraction of the price you would pay back home. Good places to hunt out a bargain are Taroudannt and Tiznit, as well as Essaouira.

Leather: top of most visitors' lists is Moroccan leather. The ultra soft, fine-grained leather known as morocco is made from goatskins, and is used for book bindings, desk sets, portfolios, wallets, purses, gloves and many other articles.

Leather jackets, suitcases, satchels and handbags are also popular. High-fashion leather clothing can be made to order in Agadir. Another favourite buy is a pair of traditional Moroccan leather slippers, or *babouches,* yellow for men and red for women.

Metalwork: you might like to buy a copper or brass tray with fine, ornate hammered designs which, along with a small folding wooden stand, makes a useful and attractive little table. The squat, narrow-spouted teapots used for making mint tea can be made of both silver and pewter – or even aluminium, so you can choose one that fits your budget.

Pottery: Fès, Meknès, Salé and Marrakech are the best places to go if you are looking for good-quality pottery. The classic souvenir is a conical couscous dish, but the choice of articles available is wide, ranging from modern plates and coffee services to beautiful antique bowls and vases.

Spices and Herbs: keen cooks will be unable to resist the heaps of fresh herbs and spices on offer in the souks. Saffron in particular is cheap by Western standards, and don't forget to ask for the 'shopkeeper's choice', called *ras el hanout*, an intriguing blend of 13 herbs and spices.

Woodwork: jars, boxes, chairs and tables made from sweet-

*M*oroccan carpets carry a wide selection of attractive, traditional Berber designs.

smelling cedar wood can be found in the Medinas of most major cities. In Essaouira, the speciality is carved and inlaid sandalwood, or *thuya*, which is made into chessboards, backgammon sets, inlaid tables and polished jewellery boxes. Buy them from the craftsmen. **91**

Sports

Swimming and Watersports: Morocco has 2,000km (1,250 miles) of coastline facing the Atlantic Ocean, with several outstanding beaches. The best are at **Asilah** and **Larache**, south of Tangier; **Témara** and the **Plage des Nations**, south and north of Rabat; and **Agadir** and **Essaouira**. It is advisable not to venture out of your depth anywhere on the Atlantic coast. If an undertow catches you it can sweep you out to sea in a matter of minutes.

Morocco's **Mediterranean beaches** are pleasant and varied, and generally free from the threat of undertow. Those backed by the Rif Mountains have only recently been developed as resorts and many of them are very attractive, most notably those around Al Hoceima. Explore the possibilities at M'diq, Cabo Negro, Smir-Restinga and Taïfor.

Surfing and **windsurfing** activities have become very popular on the breezy Atlantic coast of Morocco. Tarhazoute, just north of Agadir, and Essaouira have acquired an international reputation as two of Morocco's best sites. **Sailing** and **scuba-diving** are available in Agadir.

Fishing: Morocco offers opportunities for deep-sea angling and rock-fishing as well as surf-casting on the Atlantic and Mediterranean coasts, and freshwater angling for trout, bass and pike in the lakes and streams of the Atlas Mountains. All freshwater anglers require a permit from the Service des Eaux et Forêts (Waters and Forests Service), which also gives out information on closed seasons and local regulations. Contact the ONMT for details (see p.126).

Golf: in Morocco, golf is a royal sport – King Hassan II is a great devotee of the game. The Royal Dar-Es-Salam Club at Rabat boasts one 9-hole and two 18-hole championship golf courses, designed by Robert Trent Jones, with luxurious clubhouse facilities. There are other 18-hole courses at Mohammedia, Tangier and Marrakech, and 9-hole courses at Agadir, Cabo Negro (near Tetouan), Meknès and Casablanca. The links are open all the year round, and green fees are very reasonable.

Horse Riding: you can hire a mount in Agadir for a ride along the beach or out into the countryside, while organized treks into the High Atlas are run from the Hôtel La Roseraie at Ouirgane, near Marrakech. For further information, contact the ONMT (see p.126).

Hunting: for enthusiasts, there is a 119,000ha (295,000 acre) hunting reserve at Arbaoua, near the coast south of Larache, and smaller reserves near Marrakech, Agadir, Kabila and Benslimane. Arrangements are best made through a specialist tour operator in your home country; for details, contact the ONMT (see p.126).

*B*eginners can try windsurfing at Agadir, while the experts head for Essaouira.

Winter Sports: you can ski in the Atlas and Rif Mountains between December and April, snow conditions permitting. The biggest resort is Oukaïmeden, south of Marrakech, at an altitude of 3,200m (10,500ft); it has a few hotels, one chairlift and six tows, and equipment rental is available. There are smaller ski areas at Ifrane, near Meknès, and Ketama in the Rif. Hotel reservations are advisable at weekends.

Trekking and Mountain Biking: a number of adventure holiday companies now offer trekking and mountain-biking trips in the Atlas Mountains. The High Atlas has a number of high-level, multi-day walking routes, with accommodation in French Alpine Club mountain huts. In winter, the high peaks provide a challenging playground for all experienced mountaineers. The many unsurfaced roads and tracks that wind through the valleys provide ideal terrain for mountain bikers; the tour companies organize accommodation and provide Land Rover back-up. Contact the ONMT (see p.126).

Entertainment

NIGHTLIFE

Early evening is promenade time in all Moroccan towns, when it seems as if the entire population turns out for a stroll along the main avenue with family and friends and a chat over coffee or mint tea.

Major hotels and traditional Moroccan restaurants in the main tourist cities offer evening entertainment in the form of a Moroccan banquet, with folk music, dancing, fire-eaters, and perhaps a (decidedly un-Moroccan) belly dancer. Some of the restaurants in Fès and Marrakech are in beautiful former palaces, worth visiting for the décor alone.

In the larger cities and tourist resorts, notably Rabat, Casablanca, Marrakech, Tangier and Agadir, you will find a few European-style bars and discos.

*M*oroccans have adopted the French passion for cycle racing – the annual Tour du Maroc.

MAJOR FESTIVALS

Exact dates should be confirmed through local tourist offices.

February	*Tafraoute (near Agadir)*: popular Almond Blossom Festival.
April	*Sefrou*: Festival of Cherries – celebrating one of Sefrou's most cherished crops.
Early May	*Essaouira*: Moussem of Zaouïa el Kettania.
May-June	*El Kelaa M'Gounna (near Ouarzazate)*: Rose Petal Festival. *Marrakech*: National Folklore Festival.
Early June	*Goulimine*: Moussem of Sidi M'Hamed Benamar – attracting a large number of tribesmen from the desert. .
June	*Casablanca*: Moussem of Sidi Moussa.
July	*Chaouen*: Moussem of Outa Hammou.
Early August	*Témara (near Rabat)*: Moussem at the coastal shrine of Sidi Lahcen.
August	*Asilah*: International Arts Festival. *Rabat*: Moussem of Dar Zhirou. *Ourika Valley (near Marrakech)*: Moussem of Sitti Fatma.
Late August	*Essaouira*: Moussem of Sidi Mogdoul.
Early September	*Fès*: Moussem of Sidi Ahmed el Bernoussi. *Marrakech*: Moussem of Sidi Abdalhak ben Yasin.
Mid-September	*Marrakech*: Moussem of El Guern.
September	*Moulay Idriss (near Meknès)*: Moussem of Moulay Idriss. *Meknès*: National Fantasia Festival.

They stay open until late – ask your hotel receptionist for a recommendation. There's a casino in Marrakech's Hôtel Mamounia; dress smartly.

A Gnaoua band beats out a lively rhythm in the crowded Jema el Fna in Marrakech.

FOLKLORE AND FESTIVALS

The best possible way to experience genuine Moroccan folk music and dance, away from a tourist-oriented environment, is is to attend one of the country's many *moussems*, or religious festivals, held in honour of a local saint or holy man (*marabout*). These events attract people from far and wide to the saint's tomb for several days of festivities. There are hundreds of annual *moussems* in Morocco, ranging from local affairs to national holidays. Many are held during August and September, following the harvest. You can ask locally whether any are taking place during your stay; the most important ones are listed on the previous page.

Folk dancing is a big part of any popular festival or religious holiday. Most famous is the *guedra* dance, performed by Berber girls in the southern reaches of the country. It's a most mysterious sight – the heavily veiled dancers perform in a kneeling position (it was originally performed in low, desert tents), and slowly entrance their audience with undulating movements of the arms and hands.

The most rhytmic Moroccan dancers are descended from Sudanese slaves brought to Morocco by Arab traders. You can recognize *Gnaoua* dancers by their black-and-white costumes decorated with seashells, and by the quick and exciting beat of their drums and metal 'castanets', called *garagab*.

The most exciting of all Moroccan traditions is undoubtedly the breathtaking *fantasia*, a brilliant display of precision horsemanship, based on the traditional battle tactics of trib-

al warriors. A band of horsemen in flowing robes charges down upon the waiting spectators, long rifles twirling in the air, war cries echoing above the thunder of hooves. Then all at once, on an unseen command, they stop dead in their tracks at the edge of the crowd amid a volley of rifle shots, and then retreat as swiftly as they came. Moroccans love the spectacle of a *fantasia*, which forms part of any large festival or important *moussem*. *Fantasias* are also organized in tourist resorts in Tangier, Agadir and Marrakech.

For details of major national holidays, see p.124.

Children's Morocco

Resort hotels often lay on entertainment for children, and a beach is never far away – although Mediterranean beaches are safer than their Atlantic counterparts. Watersports are a good bet for older children, and camel treks, *fantasias* and the animation of the Jema el Fna in Marrakech will also hold their attention.

Eating Out

Morocco can boast one of the most exciting and exotic cuisines in the world, with influences derived from traditional Berber cooking, the Middle East, Andalusia and France.

Where to Eat

Eating places in Morocco can be divided into four categories. First there is the basic café-restaurant aimed mainly at local people, usually found in the Medina and often a hole-in-the-wall type place with tables out on the pavement. It serves cheap, solid fare such as kebabs, sausage, soup, salad and bread, at very low prices.

Then there are the French-style cafés and *pâtisseries* found in the *villes nouvelles* of the larger cities, where you can enjoy a croissant, cake or pastry washed down with coffee, mint tea or fruit juice. The most popular places with travellers tend to be the middle-range restaurants offering a mix of Moroccan and French dishes. This category includes the seafood restaurants on the coast, and the Italian, Chinese, Vietnamese and other international restaurants found in the larger cities.

Top of the range in terms of price and setting are the palatial establishments advertised as 'traditional Moroccan restaurants'. These are usually housed in converted mansions in the Medinas of Marrakech, Fès and Meknès, and offer banquet-type meals accompanied by a floor show of folk music and dancing. Advance reservations are essential for these places.

Meal Times

Breakfast: a traditional Moroccan breakfast consists of mint tea or coffee with bread and jam or honey, and perhaps a hard-boiled egg or some cheese and a handful of olives. City-bred Moroccans begin their day the French way, with coffee and croissants or other pastries. In a hotel the standard 'tourist' breakfast often consists of a croissant or roll, jam

*S*idewalk cafés – such as this one in Essaouira – line the main street in most Moroccan towns.

consist of soup or salad followed by two main courses, often *bstilla* and couscous, and rounded off with a dessert of fresh fruits and pastries.

and butter, with coffee, tea or hot chocolate, and is served between 7 and 9am.

Lunch and Dinner: lunch is served between noon and 3pm, and dinner between about 7 and 9pm. A formal Moroccan-style evening meal at one of the expensive Medina restaurants (see p.98) is likely to

CLASSIC MOROCCAN DISHES

Appetizers

The best-known of Moroccan soups is *harira*, a thick, peppery broth made with lentils, chick peas, mutton and tomatoes, often thickened with rice, and flavoured with lemon and tarragon. The dish is served **99**

*T*he tajine *is a rich stew of meat, vegetables and dried fruit cooked in an earthenware pot.*

onion, cucumber and green pepper, in an oil and vinegar dressing and flavoured with fresh coriander. *Merguez* is spicy beef or lamb sausage.

Briouats are small turnovers of thin pastry dough filled with *kefta* (spiced finely chopped meat), rice, almonds, sausage or fish – a kind of Moroccan samosa. They are briefly deep-fried and served hot. *Rghaïfs*, though difficult to order because of their almost unpronounceable name, comprise a variety of fillings tucked within the folds of thin, fried pancakes and served hot.

traditionally in the evening during Ramadan to break the day's fast, but you will find *harira* – it's virtually a generic term for thick soup – offered in restaurants all year round.

Other starters include *brochettes*, small cubes of lamb grilled on skewers, and *kefta*, meatballs of minced lamb with cumin and coriander, cooked on a charcoal grill, too. A *salade marocaine* (or Moroccan salad) is usually a very finely **100** chopped mixture of tomato,

Main Courses

Bstilla (*bastela*, *pastilla*) is a rich pigeon pie, a favourite local delicacy usually offered only in the more expensive restaurants because it takes a great deal of time and labour to prepare. First the pigeons are cooked, then the meat is spread in layers of paper-thin *ouarka* (flaky pastry) along with saffron, almonds, cinnamon and icing sugar. Baked to a delightful crispness, the fin-ished pie is a rich, sweet and delicious concoction.

Couscous: it is virtually impossible to spend some time Morocco without encountering the local staple, couscous. Couscous consists of a heap of steamed semolina grains topped with stewed vegetables and meat (lamb or chicken for the most part) and flavoured with herbs and spices. If you prefer, you can ask for your couscous *sans viande* (without meat), although vegetarians should note that the vegetables have probably been cooked in meat stock.

Méchoui: you have only to wander into the hungry crowd at a *moussem* to encounter a Moroccan *méchoui*. The cook digs a pit, fills it with burning charcoal, and then spit-roasts a whole lamb over the glowing embers. Alternatively, you can

enjoy lamb prepared in this way at the banquets organized for tourists in Tangier, Marrakech and Agadir.

Tajine: in Morocco a casserole or stew is called a *tajine*, after the earthenware pot in which it is traditionally prepared. The best restaurants will serve the dish in the pot, with its distinctive conical lid,

*F*resh Moroccan bread is served with a flourish in upmarket restaurants.

though it is unlikely that the chef cooked it the traditional way by burying it within a charcoal fire in the ground. The usual ingredients are lamb or chicken with vegetables or fruit, such as prunes, dates, apricots or lemon. You may see a *tajine* made with fish, identified by the name *hout tajine* on the menu. It is served with bread, which is used to mop up the delicious juices.

Fish and Seafood

Morocco's long coastline and numerous lakes and streams provide a rich catch of fish for the Moroccan table. Red mullet, dorado, sardines, sea bass and trout head the list. Fish can be used in a *tajine* or couscous, but is more often grilled or poached and served alone as a main course.

Moroccan waters also yield a fine selection of *fruits de mer*

The elaborate art of the olive merchant is on display in the narrow streets of the souk.

(seafood) – especially *poulpe* and *calamar* (octopus; squid), usually served deep-fried in a light batter. A popular delicacy is elvers (*civelles*) – baby eels the size of matchsticks – sautéed in butter and garlic and served with bread.

Desserts

When it comes to dessert, Moroccans have a very sweet tooth. Honey is a major ingredient in many familiar desserts – *briouats*, the little puffs of ultra-thin pastry described on p.100 as a starter, can also serve as a sweet when stuffed with honey and almonds. *Griouches*, twisted strips of honeyed pastry dough baked and sprinkled with sesame seeds, are popular as a last course at dinner and are also sold as a snack in the souks.

The best-known of the local after-dinner treats is *kaab el ghzal*, or *cornes de gazelle*, which means gazelle's horns. These small horn-shaped pastries are filled with almond paste and flavoured with orange-flower water.

If you yourself have a really sweet tooth, search the menu for stuffed dates (*dattes farcies*). The classic recipe calls for the best-quality dates, stuffed with a paste of ground toasted almonds, sugar and orange-flower water.

Fresh fruit is often served to round off the meal – succulent melon, figs, oranges, peaches, dates and apricots.

Drinks

Morocco's national drink is **mint tea**, or *thé à la menthe*, a delicious and refreshing drink made from an infusion of green tea with sprigs of fresh mint, and well sweetened with sugar. It is usually served in small, tulip-shaped glasses. (Tea was introduced to Morocco by British merchants in the 19th century.)

A visit to a Moroccan home wouldn't be complete without the friendly ritual of the tea-making ceremony. The honour usually falls to an important guest. The squat and curvy teapot made of silver, pewter or enamel is rinsed with boiling **103**

Imported wines and spirits are expensive – local wines are very palatable and better value.

which is then tasted for sweetness, more sugar is added if necessary, and the tea, finally, is served.

Coffee is available in all French-style cafés, and is usually served strong, black and sweet (*café noir*). If you want a little milk added to the brew, ask for *café cassé*, or *café au lait* for a lot of milk.

Although the consumption of **alcohol** is forbidden by Islamic law, wine, beer and spirits are available quite freely to visitors in the hotels, bars and restaurants of the *villes nouvelles* and coastal resorts.

Mineral water (*eau minérale*) is available in all restaurants, either still (*non gazeuse*) or sparkling (*gazeuse*).

Moroccan **wines** are of a high standard, and well worth trying. In the major cities, even the more modest restaurants will have a few good local wines to choose from, and the better places will have quite a varied selection.

The home-brewed **beers**, Stork and Flag, are nothing special, but are much cheaper than imported brands.

water and emptied. Green tea and a sprig of fresh mint are then jammed into the pot and scalded with a small amount of boiling water, which is then swished around and poured away. Sugar is now added, and the pot filled with boiling water from a copper kettle. It is allowed to infuse for a few minutes then the teapot is held high and a glass filled, and the contents poured back into the **104** pot. A further glass is filled

Prices of most drinks are moderate, particularly mineral water, mint tea and soft drinks, but imported wine and spirits are relatively expensive and can add considerably to the bill.

To Help You Order...

Could we have a table for …, please?	**Pouvons-nous avoir une table pour …, s'il vous plaît?**
Do you have a set menu?	**Avez-vous un menu?**
Do you have any vegetarian dishes?	**Avez-vous (un) des plat(s) végétarien(s)?**
I'd like a/an/some …	**J'aimerais …**

English	French	English	French
beer	**une bière**	napkin	**une serviette**
bread	**du pain**	oil	**de l'huile**
butter	**du beurre**	pepper	**du poivre**
chicken	**du poulet**	potatoes	**pommes de terre**
coffee	**un café**		
dessert	**un dessert**	rice	**du riz**
duck	**du canard**	salad	**de la salade**
eggs	**des œufs**	salt	**du sel**
fish	**du poisson**	sandwich	**un sandwich**
fork	**une fourchette**	seafood	**fruits de mer**
fruit	**des fruits**	soup	**de la soupe**
glass	**un verre**	spoon	**une cuiller**
ice-cream	**une glace**	stew	**une tajine**
knife	**un couteau**	sugar	**du sucre**
lemon	**du citron**	tea (mint)	**du thé (à la menthe)**
meat	**de la viande**		
menu	**la carte**	vegetables	**des légumes**
milk	**du lait**	vinegar	**du vinaigre**
mineral water (fizzy)	**de l'eau minérale (gazeuse)**	water (iced)	**de l'eau (glacée)**
mustard	**de la moutarde**	wine	**du vin**

...and Read the Menu

agneau	lamb	**fraise**	strawberry
ail	garlic	**fromage**	cheese
ananas	pineapple	**(de chèvre)**	(goat's)
artichaut	artichoke	**gâteau**	cake
asperge	asparagus	**ghoraiba**	sweet biscuits
aubergine	aubergine	**haloua**	halva
	(eggplant)	**homard**	lobster
bar	bass	**huîtres**	oysters
biftek	beefsteak	**langouste**	spiny lobster
bœuf	beef	**maquereau**	mackerel
boulettes	meatballs	**Merguez**	spicy sausage
brochette	skewered meat	**morue**	codfish
canard	duck	**moules**	mussels
carottes	carrots	**navet**	turnip
champignons	mushrooms	**noix**	nuts
chou	cabbage	**nouilles**	noodles
chou-fleur	cauliflower	**œufs**	eggs
concombre	cucumber	**pamplemousse**	grapefruit
confiture	jam	**pêches**	peaches
côtelette	chops	**persil**	parsley
courge,	courgette	**petits pois**	peas
courgette	zucchini, squash	**poire**	pear
crevettes	shrimps	**pois chiches**	chick peas
dattes	dates	**pomme**	apple
daurade	sea bream	**poulet**	chicken
écrevisses	crayfish	**raisins**	grapes
épinards	spinach	**rognon**	kidney
escargots	snails	**rouget**	red mullet
faisan	pheasant	**saumon**	saumon
figues	figs	**thon**	tuna
flan	custard	**truite**	trout
foie	liver	**vin**	wine

BLUEPRINT
for a
Perfect Trip

An A-Z Summary of Practical Information

> Listed after most main entries is an appropriate French translation, usually in the singular. You'll find this vocabulary useful when asking for information or assistance.

A

ACCOMMODATION (*logement; hôtel*)
(See also CAMPING on p.110, YOUTH HOSTELS on p.131 and the list of RECOMMENDED HOTELS starting on p.66)
When it comes to hotels, Morocco is a bargain for the independent traveller. Accommodation ranges from the very cheap, unclassified hotels of the Medina to luxury, five-star international establishments. The official grading system runs from one to five stars, with each grade (except five-star) subdivided into 'A' and 'B'. The lower grades offer only basic facilities – smelly toilets, sagging mattresses and no towels or hot water – but are very cheap by Western standards. If you are looking for European levels of comfort and service, then choose at least a three-star A hotel.

By law, prices must be displayed in reception and in the rooms. The quoted rates usually include VAT at 14% (TVA in French), but other local taxes – Taxe Promotion Touristique (TPT) and Taxe de Séjour (TS) – may add another 5 to 12dh per night to your bill. Check also whether breakfast is included. Book ahead during the peak periods of August, Christmas/New Year and Easter.

A list of hotels rated by the Moroccan National Tourist Office is available from their overseas offices (see TOURIST INFORMATION OFFICES on p.126).

AIRPORTS (aéroport)

Morocco's main international airports are at Casablanca, Tangier, Agadir and Marrakech. **Casablanca** is served by Mohammed V Airport, 30km (18 miles) to the south of the city, with all the facilities you would expect of a major international airport – currency exchange, bank, post office, car hire, restaurants and duty-free shops. There is a rail link between the airport and central Casablanca, with connections to Rabat; trains run hourly between 8.30am and 10.30pm, and take 20 minutes to Casablanca-Voyageurs station, 30 minutes to Casablanca-Port (more convenient for the city centre). A shuttle bus runs between the airport and the CTM bus station downtown, with services hourly between 6am and 11pm; journey time is 40 minutes. *Grand taxis* (see TRANSPORT on p.127) are also available.

Agadir is served by the bright, modern and efficient Al Massira Airport, situated 25km (15 miles) to the east of the resort. Passengers on charter flights will be met by the holiday company's coach for the 30-minute trip into town. Otherwise, you can take the hourly airport bus, or a *grand taxi*.

Tangier Airport is 15km (9 miles) southwest of the city. If you are not on a charter flight, which will be met by a coach, then you will have to take a taxi. **Marrakech** Airport lies about 5km (3 miles) southwest of the city. A taxi is the best way of getting into town, but make sure you negotiate the fare with the driver before getting in.

B

BICYCLE and MOPED RENTAL
(location de bicyclettes/motos)

Bicycles and mopeds can be rented in Agadir, Taroudannt, Ouarzazate and Zagora. Inspect the bike carefully before taking it, as you will be responsible for repairing if it breaks down. Check that the quoted rates for mopeds include tax and insurance. Remember that mopeds and scooters are potentially very dangerous. Go slowly and keep to quiet back roads until you get the hang of it – every year there are many bad accidents involving tourists on two wheels.

CAMPING (le camping)

Campsites can be found in most of the popular tourist areas of Morocco, especially along the Atlantic coast – the local tourist information office will have details of nearby sites. Facilities vary widely, from very basic (a patch of bare earth with a toilet block) to shaded, comfortable sites with electricity hook-up, showers, laundry, swimming pool, bar and restaurant. Prices are generally low by European standards. A list of official sites can be obtained from Moroccan National Tourist Offices (see TOURIST INFORMATION OFFICES on p.126). Camping outside of official sites is permitted provided you obtain permission from the landowner.

CAR RENTAL (location de voitures)
(See also DRIVING on p.114)

Although expensive by European and North American standards, renting a car is an ideal way of discovering the Moroccan landscape. A car gives you the freedom to travel at your own pace, and to explore places inaccessible by public transport. There are numerous car hire firms in the major cities and tourist resorts; local firms often charge a great deal less than the big international chains but rates vary considerably, and you should shop around for the lowest price. Always be wary of any agency recommended by a 'guide'; he is bound to be on commission.

The best rates are usually to be had by booking and paying for your car before you leave home, either directly through an international rental company or as part of a fly-drive package deal. Check that the quoted rate includes Collision Damage Waiver, unlimited mileage, and tax (currently 19% in Morocco), as these can considerably increase the cost.

You must be over 21 to rent a car, and you will need a full driver's licence (EU model) which you must have held for a minimum of 12 months, your passport, and a major credit card – cash deposits are prohibitively large.

CLIMATE and CLOTHING

A Mediterranean climate with hot, dry summers and mild, rainy winters extends over the northern and central parts of the country, giving way to a semi-arid desert climate south of the Atlas Mountains. The months of May to September are the best time to visit the coastal resorts and the north of the country, with consistent sunshine and high temperatures, though it can be uncomfortably hot in inland cities like Fès and Meknès.

Winter is the time to visit if you intend exploring the deep south – Marrakech, Ouarzazate and Zagora are all popular winter-sun destinations. Remember, however, that the difference in temperature between day and night in the desert can be huge. Take along some warm clothes for the evenings.

The following **chart** shows the average daily maximum temperature for each month in Tangier and Agadir:

	J	F	M	A	M	J	J	A	S	O	N	D
Tangier °C	15	16	17	19	21	24	26	27	25	22	18	16
Tangier °F	59	61	63	66	70	75	79	81	77	72	64	61
Agadir °C	20	21	23	23	24	26	27	27	27	26	24	21
Agadir °F	68	70	73	73	75	79	81	81	81	79	75	70

Clothing. From June to September the days are always hot – lightweight cotton clothes are the most comfortable choice – but evenings sometimes turn cool, so take along a jacket or sweater. Remember also to take a couple of long-sleeved shirts and a sunhat to protect against the strong midday sunshine, and plenty of suntan lotion with a high protection factor. During the rest of the year a light jacket and a raincoat or umbrella will come in handy, while a warm coat for desert nights is essential.

Respectable clothing should, of course, be worn when visiting mosques and other Islamic monuments. Topless sunbathing is permitted only in private hotel grounds, not on public beaches. (See also WOMEN TRAVELLERS on p.131.)

COMMUNICATIONS (See also TIME DIFFERENCES on p.126)

Post Offices (*bureau de poste*). Post offices handle mail, parcels, telegrams and telephone calls; they are marked by a yellow sign with the letters 'PTT'. If you want to buy stamps, look for the counter marked '*timbres*'. Hours are generally 8.30am to 6.30pm Monday to Friday, closed weekends (in smaller towns there may be a break from noon to 3pm). Larger cities have a *permanence* counter which stays open 24 hours a day. (See also OPENING HOURS on p.123.) Postage stamps are also on sale at tobacconists' kiosks (*tabacs*) and hotel desks, and at tourist shops that sell postcards.

Poste restante (general delivery). If you don't know ahead of time where you'll be staying, you can have your mail addressed to you c/o Poste Restante in whichever town is most convenient, with your surname underlined, eg:

Mr John <u>Smith</u>
Poste Restante
Casablanca
Morocco

It will be held for you at the main post office, but delays are common and there can be confusion with the filing of European names – if you are expecting mail and there is nothing under your surname, ask the staff to check your first name, and even 'M' for Mr/Mrs/Ms. Take your passport along as identification.

Telephones (*téléphone*). Domestic and international telephone calls can be made from public telephones in the main post office, or from phone boxes on the street (*cabines*), which take 1dh and 5dh coins. In the larger cities you will also find card phones – the cards can usually be bought at a nearby news-stand or kiosk.

To make a call within **Morocco**, lift the receiver, insert your coins, and simply dial the number, including the two-digit area code for calls outside the city you are calling from. The ringing tone is a single long tone.

To make an **international call**, dial 00 and wait for a second tone, then dial the country code (44 for the UK, 353 for Ireland, 1 for the

USA and Canada) and the full number, including the area code minus the initial zero. To make a **reverse-charge** (collect) call, dial 12 for the international operator, and ask to be connected to an operator in your home country.

COMPLAINTS (*réclamation*)

Complaints should first be made to the management of the establishment involved. If satisfaction is not obtained, ask to be given the complaints book (*livre des réclamations*); the law requires that all hotels, restaurants and official guides provide one. Usually, a demand for the complaints book will settle the matter; if not, then seek advice from the local tourist office.

To avoid problems, always establish a price in advance, especially when dealing with guides, taxi drivers and porters at stations.

CRIME (See also EMERGENCIES on p.117 and POLICE on p.124)

Morocco has a very low crime rate. Theft from tourists is rare, and physical assault almost unheard of. Nevertheless, you should take the usual precautions against theft, especially in the larger cities – don't carry large amounts of cash; leave your valuables in the hotel safe, not in your room; and beware of pickpockets in crowded areas. Never leave your bags or valuables on view in a parked car – take them with you or lock them in the boot. Any theft or loss must be reported immediately to the police in order to comply with your travel insurance. If your passport is lost or stolen, you should also inform your consulate (see EMBASSIES AND CONSULATES on p.000).

CUSTOMS (*douane*) and ENTRY FORMALITIES

Citizens of the UK, Republic of Ireland, USA, Canada, Australia and New Zealand need only a full passport for visits of up to 90 days (a British Visitor's Passport is not acceptable); the passport must be valid for a minimum of three months after the date you arrive. Children who are travelling on their parents' passport must have their photographs attached to the passport – if you do not comply with this requirement, you may be refused entry.

Visas. Visas are not required for stays of less than 90 days. (Visa regulations change from time to time, however, and should be confirmed through your travel agent.)

Duty-free allowance. When getting into Morocco and upon your return home, restrictions are as follows. **Morocco**: 200 cigarettes or 50 cigars or 400g of tobacco, 1l of wine and 1l spirits; **Australia**: 250 cigarettes or 250g tobacco, 1l alcohol; **Canada**: 200 cigarettes and 50 cigars and 400g tobacco, 1.1l wine or spirits or 8.5l beer; **New Zealand**: 200 cigarettes or 50 cigars or 250g tobacco, 4.5l wine or beer and 1.1l spirits; **Republic of Ireland**: 200 cigarettes or 50 cigars or 250g tobacco, 2l wine or 1l spirits; **South Africa**: 400 cigarettes and 50 cigars and 250g tobacco, 2l wine and 1l spirits; **UK**: 200 cigarettes or 50 cigars or 250g tobacco, 2l wine or 1l spirits; **USA**: 200 cigarettes or 50 cigars or 2kg tobacco, 1l of wine or spirits.

Currency restrictions. You can take as much foreign currency as you like into or out of the country, but amounts in excess of 15,000 dirhams equivalent must be declared on entry. It is illegal to import or export Moroccan dirhams.

D

DRIVING IN MOROCCO (See also CAR RENTAL on p.110)
Motorists planning to take their own vehicle into Morocco will need a full driver's licence, an international motor insurance certificate and Green Card, and a vehicle registration document. An official nationality plate must be displayed near the rear number plate, and headlamp beams must be adjusted for driving on the right. Full details are available from your insurance company.

The use of seat belts in both front and back seats is obligatory; fines for non-compliance are stiff. A red warning triangle must be carried. Motorcycle riders and their passengers must wear crash helmets. Note that the minimum legal age for driving in Morocco is 21.

Driving conditions. Drive on the right, and pass on the left. Speed
limits are 100kph (60mph) on highways, and 40 or 50kph (25 or

30mph) in towns and cities. Traffic joining a road from the right has priority, unless signs or markings indicate otherwise. Most importantly, this means that cars already on a roundabout must give way to those joining it. One local quirk you should be prepared for is that drivers making a left turn on a two-lane road often move over to the wrong side of the road before turning – this can be rather disconcerting if you are travelling in the opposite direction.

Driving conditions outside the cities are generally good on the main routes, with long, straight stretches and little traffic. Minor roads are often wide enough for one vehicle only, and you will have to move on to the gravel shoulder to pass oncoming traffic. You should look out for pedestrians, donkey carts and mopeds, especially near towns, where they often wander across the road without any apparent concern for their own safety. They also make driving after dark particularly hazardous.

If you plan to wander off the main routes, a reliable road map is essential. Many minor roads are unsurfaced, and should not be attempted without a four-wheel-drive vehicle and a local guide. Remember, too, that many of the roads across the Atlas Mountains are high enough to be blocked by snow in the winter.

Road signs. Most road signs use the standard European pictographs, and directional signs are given in both French and Arabic. Here is a list of the more common written signs:

Arrêt	Stop
Attention	Caution
Attention Travaux	Caution – road works
Cédez	Give way, yield
Crue	Road liable to flood
Défense de stationner	No parking
Déviation	Diversion, detour
Lentement	Slow
Serrez à droite	Keep right
Virages	Bends, curves

Petrol. Petrol (*essence*) and diesel (*gas-oil*) are easily obtained. There are plenty of service stations in and around towns, but they can be few and far between in the south, so always fill up at the beginning of the day when you are travelling in the more remote areas. Most cars take premium grade (*super*); lead-free petrol (*sans-plomb*) is available only in the larger towns.

Parking. In the centre of most large towns and cities, parking is controlled by *gardiens* – attendants in blue coats, often with a brass badge, who will guide you into a space, perhaps clean your windscreen, and claim a small fee. One or two dirhams is normal; there is no set charge. *Gardiens* are licensed by the local town council, so don't try to avoid paying – they are not hustlers.

Traffic police. Motorcycle police patrol the main highways, and occasionally set up checkpoints. You may be asked to show your passport and registration or car hire documents, but once the officer realizes you are a tourist he will usually just wave you on.

Breakdown. In most towns there should be no problem finding a mechanic to carry out minor repairs. However, if you break down in the more remote parts of the country you will probably have to rely on assistance from passing cars, or carry out repairs yourself. If you have a rental car, follow the procedure laid down by the rental company, and check with them before setting off.

Distance

Fluid measures

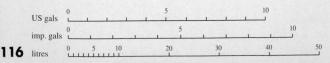

ELECTRIC CURRENT

220V/50Hz AC is standard, but older installations of 110V can still be found; check before plugging in. An adaptor for continental-style two-pin sockets will be needed, and American 110V appliances will also require a transformer.

EMBASSIES and CONSULATES (ambassade/consulat)

Canada: *embassy*: 13 bis, rue Joafar Assadik, Agdal, Rabat, tel. (07) 77.14.76.

S. Africa: *SA Interest Office*: 34, rue Saadians, Rabat; tel. (07) 70.67.60.

UK: *embassy*: 17, boulevard de la Tour Hassan, Rabat, tel. (07) 72.09.05.
consulates: 60, boulevard d'Anfa, Casablanca, tel. (02) 22.16.53/22.17.41; 9, rue Amérique du Sud, Tangier, tel. (09) 93.58.95.

USA: *embassy*: 2, avenue de Marrakech, Rabat, tel. (07) 76.22.65.
consulate: 8, boulevard Moulay Youssef, Casablanca, tel. (02) 26.45.50/22.41.49.

EMERGENCIES (See also POLICE on p.124)

Police	**19**
Ambulance	**15**
Fire	**15**

ETIQUETTE

The people of Morocco are by nature friendly, courteous and immensely hospitable – do not allow the touts and hustlers in places like Tangier and Marrakech to influence your opinion of Moroccans in general. Moroccans have a tradition of tolerance and respect for **117** others, and you should reciprocate by showing a similar respect for local customs and sensibilities.

It is customary to shake hands on meeting, and then to place your right hand briefly over your heart. If you are invited into a Moroccan home don't forget to remove your shoes before entering. Most important of all is dress – away from the beach, you should dress modestly (see also WOMEN TRAVELLERS on p.131).

The king is held in great respect – never make any jokes or frivolous comments about the monarch or show disrespect to the national flag. Non-Muslims are forbidden to enter mosques, *koubbas* (shrines) and most other Islamic monuments, except the courtyard of Moulay Ismaïl's tomb in Meknès, the Bou Inania Medersa in Fès and the Mausoleum of Mohammed V in Rabat. If you plan to visit any of these you should dress conservatively.

G

GUIDES and TOURS (*guide/excursion*)

Official, English-speaking guides can be hired through the local tourist office (see TOURIST INFORMATION OFFICES on p.126) and the better hotels. They are usually friendly and knowledgeable, and can prove invaluable if time is limited, especially for navigating the labyrinthine Medinas of Fès and Marrakech.

Official guides carry a brass ID badge, unlike the many unofficial 'guides' and hustlers who hang around the Medina gates in tourist towns. These can be very persistent in their attentions – if you genuinely don't want their services be firm and polite. If you do decide to engage one, even if it's only to get the others off your back, make sure you agree in advance *exactly* what you want to see, and the price to be paid (about half the cost of an official guide). They will invariably try to take you into a shop, probably under the pretext of showing you an 'exhibition' or 'museum' of carpets or crafts, or taking some mint tea with a friend. This is always a lie, intended to get you inside a shop where they can earn commission from the owner. If you don't want to buy anything, politely insist on not going in.

LANGUAGE

The official language of Morocco is Arabic, but a large proportion of the population, especially in the cities, is bilingual in Arabic and French; most signs and street names are bilingual, too. If you can get by in French you should have no communication problems anywhere except in remote Berber villages, where the original Berber language is still spoken. Although written Arabic is the same throughout the Arab world, the spoken dialect of Moroccan Arabic is quite distinctive, and travellers who have learned the Arabic of the Middle East will struggle to get by.

Although Moroccans will not expect you to know any Arabic, and will always greet you in French or English, it is polite to learn at least a few basic phrases. Refer to the cover of this guide for some useful expressions. The Berlitz phrase books FRENCH FOR TRAVELLERS and ARABIC FOR TRAVELLERS will cover most situations you are likely to encounter in Morocco.

DAYS OF THE WEEK

Monday	**lundi**	Friday	**vendredi**
Tuesday	**mardi**	Saturday	**samedi**
Wednesday	**mercredi**	Sunday	**dimanche**
Thursday	**jeudi**		

NUMBERS

1	**un, une**	11	**onze**	21	**vingt et un**
2	**deux**	12	**douze**	30	**trente**
3	**trois**	13	**treize**	40	**quarante**
4	**quatre**	14	**quatorze**	50	**cinquante**
5	**cinq**	15	**quinze**	60	**soixante**
6	**six**	16	**seize**	70	**soixante-dix**
7	**sept**	17	**dix-sept**	80	**quatre-vingt**
8	**huit**	18	**dix-huit**	90	**quatre-vingt-dix**
9	**neuf**	19	**dix-neuf**	100	**cent**
10	**dix**	20	**vingt**	1,000	**mille**

LAUNDRY (*blanchissage*)

Your hotel will be able to provide a laundry service, even if you are staying in a modest one-star establishment (washing must be handed in before noon for return the following morning). There are no coin-operated launderettes where you can wash your clothes yourself.

LOST PROPERTY (*objets trouvés*) (See also CRIME on p.113)

Ask for advice from your hotel receptionist or the local tourist office before contacting the police. For items left behind on public transport, ask your hotel receptionist to telephone the bus or train station or taxi company.

MEDIA

Newspapers and Magazines (*journal/revue*). Locally produced French-language publications include *Le Matin du Sahara*, *L'Opinion* and *Maroc Soir*, all of which provide a thin diet of North African and international news and sport. The French dailies *Le Monde* and *Le Figaro*, and the *International Herald Tribune* are also widely available on city news-stands. British newspapers can be found a day or two after publication in the larger cities and resorts.

Radio and Television (*radio/télévision*). If you bring along a short-wave radio you will be able to pick up the English-language broadcasts of the BBC World Service and Voice of America. Otherwise, you can listen to local stations, which offer a choice of traditional Moroccan music, or news, sport and current affairs in Arabic.

You will find a TV supplied in the more expensive hotels, generally four-star and upward. The two Moroccan TV channels broadcast in Arabic, but the evening news is repeated in French and Spanish. The better hotels also have satellite TV with the French channel TV5, and occasionally Sky, CNN, MTV and Superchannel.

MEDICAL CARE (See also EMERGENCIES on p.117)

There is no free health care for visitors to Morocco. All medical services must be paid for, and you should not leave home without adequate insurance.

The main health hazards in Morocco are contaminated food and water, and the sun. Sunburn can seriously ruin your holiday. Travellers' diarrhoea can be avoided by eating only freshly cooked food and drinking only bottled water and canned or bottled drinks (without ice). Avoid restaurants that look dirty, food from street stalls, undercooked meat, salads and fruit (except fruit you can peel yourself), dairy products and tap water. The standards of hygiene in most tourist hotels and restaurants are usually quite adequate.

For minor ailments, seek advice from the local **pharmacy**. These are usually open during normal shopping hours. After hours, at least one per town remains open all night, called the *pharmacie de service* or *pharmacie de nuit*; its location is posted in the window of all other pharmacies.

Vaccinations. There are no compulsory immunization requirements for entry into Morocco. Inoculations for tetanus, polio, typhoid and hepatitis-A are recommended, especially for independent travellers who intend 'roughing it' in rural areas. There is also a malaria risk in the south of the country, although urban areas are safe. A course of anti-malarial tablets is recommended for anyone planning to travel extensively in the south.

MONEY MATTERS

Currency (*monnaie*). The unit of currency is the dirham (dh), which is divided into 100 centimes. Centimes are occasionally referred to as francs. Notes come in denominations of 10dh, 50dh and 100dh, and coins in 5, 10, 20 and 50 centimes, 1dh and 5dh.

The dirham is a soft currency, and the exchange rate is controlled by the government, so there's no point shopping around for the best rate – they're all the same. (See also CUSTOMS AND ENTRY FORMALITIES on p.113.)

Banks and currency exchange (*banque*; *change*). Banks are generally open 8.30 to 11.30am (2pm in summer) and 3 to 4.30pm Monday to Friday, but often won't exchange currency before 9.30am. The most efficient banks are the Bank Al-Maghrib, the BMCE and the Société Générale Marocaine de Banques. The usual procedure is for the clerk to fill out the forms at the counter, then give you a receipt or token which you take to the cashier (*la caisse*) where you pick up your cash. This involves queuing twice, and changing money can prove to be a time-consuming business.

In the more popular tourist resorts like Marrakech and Agadir you will find exchange booths that open independently of the banks, often open 8am to 8pm including weekends.

Traveller's cheques and credit cards (*chèque de voyages*; *cartes de crédit*). These are generally accepted at the banks mentioned above, though smaller branches may refuse to cash them and will direct you elsewhere. You will need your passport, and occasionally the purchase receipts too; no commission is charged. It is worth bringing enough hard cash for the first few days, as the exchange offices at airports and ferry terminals are notorious for being closed or 'out of money'. You can exchange cash easily in most hotels and tourist shops.

Major credit and charge cards are accepted in the more expensive hotels (three-star and above) and restaurants in the larger cities, and by tourist shops and car hire firms.

PLANNING YOUR BUDGET

To give you an idea of what to expect, here's a list of prices in Moroccan dirhams (dh). These can only be regarded as approximate, as inflation continues to push prices up.

Airport transfer. Casablanca: train 35dh; bus 20dh; taxi 200dh. Agadir: bus 12dh; taxi 100dh. Tangier: taxi 70dh. Marrakech: taxi 60dh.

Bicycle and moped hire. Rates for bicycles are negotiable, around 5dh/hour. Motorbikes (125cc) are available in Agadir for 150dh/day.

Buses. City buses have a flat fare of 1.60-2dh. Long-distance coach, one way: Casablanca-Marrakech 60dh; Marrakech-Ouarzazate 54dh.

Camping. Around 12-45dh per person per night, plus the same again for a car, caravan or camper-van.

Entertainment. Nightclub admission (including first drink), 120dh.

Guides. Official guides hired through the local tourist office charge 100dh/half-day.

Hotels (double room with bath, approximate price including taxes). One-star 110dh; two-star 160dh; three-star 250dh; four-star 450dh; five-star from 600dh up.

Meals and drinks. Meals (in four-star hotel): breakfast 40dh, set-menu dinner 150dh; (in two-star hotel) breakfast 20dh, set-menu dinner 90dh. Drinks (in pavement café): soft drinks 4-6dh, coffee 4dh, mint tea 3.50dh, large bottle of mineral water 5dh, bottle of wine 70dh.

Sightseeing. Admission to museums and historic buildings is 10dh.

Taxis. The proper fare for a cross-town trip in a *petit taxi* is about 10dh, but you will probably be asked for 20 or 30dh; negotiate a price before getting in.

Telephone calls. The cost of a three-minute international call to the UK is 54dh, to the USA 180dh.

Trains. Adult single, second class (first class is about 30% more): Tangier-Rabat 81dh; Rabat-Fès 62.50dh; Rabat-Marrakech 92dh.

Youth hostels. 15-25dh per person per night.

OPENING HOURS (*heure d'ouverture*)

Banks. 8.30 to 11.30am (2pm in summer) and 3 to 4.30pm Monday to Friday.

Currency-exchange desks. 8am to 8pm daily in popular resorts like Agadir and Marrakech.

Museums. 8.30am to 12.30pm and 2.30 to 6pm, closed Tuesday.

Post offices. 8.30am to 6.30pm, Monday to Friday (in smaller towns there may be a break from noon to 3pm).

Shops. 8.30am to noon and 2.30 to 6.30pm, Monday to Saturday.

P

PHOTOGRAPHY (*photographie*)

Major brands of film are widely available, but more expensive than in the UK, so stock up before you leave. Photo shops in major cities and resorts can process your colour prints in 24 to 48 hours at reasonable prices. Protect your film from the effects of heat, and never leave a camera or film lying in direct sunlight. The use of flash or tripod is forbidden in some museums, so always check before snapping away.

You should be aware that photogenic water-sellers and other characters in tourist haunts will expect and demand payment for allowing you to take their picture. Also, if you want to take photos of people outside the main tourist resorts, ask their permission first – many country people object to having their picture taken. Finally, don't take pictures of police or soldiersor military installations.

POLICE (*police*) (See also EMERGENCIES on p.117)

Morocco's civil police wear grey uniforms and are known as the *Sûreté Nationale*; individual officers are called *gendarmes*. There is a police station (*poste de police* or *gendarmerie*) in most towns. If you want to report a crime, it is a good idea to get a fluent French or Arabic speaker to help you – your hotel or the local tourist office may be able to help. The *Sûreté* also patrol the highways and man traffic checkpoints (see also DRIVING IN MOROCCO on p.114).

PUBLIC HOLIDAYS (*jour férié*)

There are two kinds of public holiday in Morocco – secular holidays, which occur on the same date each year, and religious holidays, which are calculated by the Islamic authorities according to the lunar calendar, and thus occur about 11 days earlier each year. Banks, post offices, government offices and many other businesses will be closed on the following secular holidays:

1 January	*Nouvel An*	New Year's Day
3 March	*Fête du Trône*	Feast of the Throne
1 May	*Fête du Travail*	Labour Day
6 November	*Anniversaire de la Marche Verte*	Anniversary of the Green March
18 November	*Fête de l'Indépendance*	Independence Day

The following religious holidays are marked by two days off. Public transport may run with reduced services. The dates given are the approximate dates for 1995; these will fall roughly 11 days earlier with each succeeding year:

1 March	*Aïd es-Seghir*	'Little Feast', the end of the month of Ramadan
10 May	*Aïd el-Kebir*	'Great Feast', commemorating the sacrifice of Abraham
5 July	*Moharem*	Muslim New Year
18 August	*Mouloud*	Birthday of the Prophet Mohammed

Ramadan occupies the four weeks preceding *Aïd es-Seghir*.

R

RELIGION

Morocco is a Muslim country but is very tolerant of other religions. Christians account for about 1% of the population; there are Roman Catholic churches in most large towns and Anglican churches in Tangier, Rabat and Casablanca. Jewish synagogues can also be found in the main cities. Details of local religious services can be obtained from the local tourist office (see TOURIST INFORMATION OFFICES on p.126).

TIME DIFFERENCES

Morocco runs on GMT all year round. The following table shows the time differences in various cities in summer.

New York	London	**Morocco**	Sydney	Los Angeles
7am	1pm	**noon**	10pm	4am

TIPPING

It is customary to offer a tip (*pourboire*) for services rendered. A couple of dirhams is the norm for café waiters, porters, parking attendants (*gardiens* – see Driving in Morocco on p.114), petrol pump attendants, and the attendants at monuments and museums, while restaurant waiters expect 5dh on top of any service charge. If a taxi driver uses his meter, then tip around 10-15% of the fare; if you agree a price beforehand (much more likely), nothing extra will be expected.

TOURIST INFORMATION OFFICES

(*office de tourisme; syndicat d'initiative*)

The Moroccan National Tourist Office (*Office National Marocain de Tourisme*, or *ONMT*) has its head office in Rabat (see below), and branches in cities and tourist resorts throughout the country. The staff can help with general inquiries, advise on local accommodation, and provide official guides and interpreters, but they rarely have much in the way of maps, literature and detailed information. The principal offices are listed below:

Rabat: Head Office, 22, avenue d'Alger; tel. (07) 73.05.62.

Agadir: Unit A, place Prince Héritier Sidi Mohammed (the main shopping centre); tel. (08) 82.28.94.

Casablanca: 55, rue Omar Slaoui; tel. (02) 27.11.77/27.95.33.

Fès: Place de la Résistance; tel. (05) 62.34.60/62.62.79.

Marrakech: Place Abdelmoumen Ben Ali; tel. (04) 44.88.89.

Meknès: Place Administrative; tel. (05) 52.44.26.

Tangier: 29, boulevard Pasteur; tel. (09) 67.27.37.

Opening hours are generally 8.30am to noon and 2.30 to 6.30pm, closed Saturday afternoon and Sunday. Most towns also have a *Syndicat d'Initiative*, an information office run by the local authorities.

The ONMT maintains a number of overseas offices, where you can obtain information, including lists of hotels and campsites, before you leave home.

In Canada: Suite 1460, 2001 rue Université, Montreal H3A 2A6; tel. (514) 842 8111.

In the UK: 205 Regent Street, London W1R 7DE; tel. (071) 437 0073.

In the USA: Suite 1201, 20 East 46th Street, New York NY 10017, tel. (212) 557 2520; 421 North Rodeo Drive, Beverly Hills, Los Angeles CA 90210, tel. (213) 271 8939; PO Box 22663, Lake Buena Vista, Orlando FLA 32830, tel. (407) 827 5337.

TRANSPORT

Buses. Two national coach lines serve almost the entire country – CTM-LN services run to most towns, while ONCF (owned by the state railways) run express services linking railway stations to outlying settlements. The national networks are supplemented by a number of local, private companies, notably SATAS in the south. Except on the express services, which have air-conditioning and videos, bus travel can be rather uncomfortable, especially over long distances; if you have a choice, take the train. Information on routes and departure times is available at tourist information offices as well as at the main bus stations.

Grands Taxis. A faster and slightly more comfortable alternative to the bus for shorter journeys between towns is the *grand taxi*. This is a large saloon or estate car seating six passengers, which shuttles back and forth along a set route. There are no fixed departure times; the taxi departs as soon as all the seats are full. To find a place, you simply turn up at the 'terminal' (the tourist office or your hotel will tell **127**

you where) and ask around the drivers. Fares are per person for a full car; ask other passengers (or your hotel receptionist) what the standard fare is if you want to avoid being overcharged.

Petits Taxis. These are small cars seating only three passengers, which operate as city taxis for short trips within town. They can be hailed in the street or picked up at a rank, and in the larger cities can be ordered by telephone. They have meters but, as the drivers tend to forget to switch them on for foreigners, you should negotiate the fare before getting in. Fares are increased by 50% after dark but are still very cheap by European standards.

Trains. The national rail company, the ONCFM (*Office National des Chemins de Fer du Maroc*), maintains a limited but efficient rail network extending from Tangier south to Marrakech and east to Oujda at the Algerian border, linking Fès, Meknès, Rabat and Casablanca. Mainline trains are modern, comfortable and inexpensive. Where possible, choose a *rapide* service, as these are faster and more comfortable than the *ordinaire* trains. A luxury, air-conditioned express service runs hourly between Casablanca, Rabat and Kenitra.

TRAVELLERS WITH DISABILITIES

As yet, there are very few facilities for disabled travellers in Morocco. Getting around the city centres, especially the medinas, in a wheelchair is difficult if not impossible, and most public transport is inaccessible. Some of the more modern beach hotels in Tangier and Agadir, however, do have wheelchair access. Make enquiries through a tour operator, stating your exact needs, before booking.

TRAVELLING TO MOROCCO

BY AIR

Scheduled flights
From the UK and Ireland: The national airline, Royal Air Maroc, offers daily flights from London Heathrow to Casablanca, Agadir, Marrakech and Tangier, with connecting services to Fès, Ouarzazate, Tetouan and many other places. For details, tel. (071) 439 4361.

British Airways flies four times a week from Heathrow to Casablanca, twice weekly to Tangier, and twice weekly from Gatwick to Marrakech. There are no direct flights from Dublin; you will have to transit via London or Paris.

From the USA and Canada: Royal Air Maroc has direct flights from New York (twice weekly) and Montreal (once a week) to Casablanca. Alternatively, you can fly to Morocco via London, Paris, Amsterdam or Madrid on a daily basis.

Charter flights and package tours
From the UK and Republic of Ireland: Charter flights are available from Manchester, Gatwick and Dublin to Agadir, and from Gatwick to Tangier. Most travel companies offer two-centre holidays, and an increasingly popular deal is the adventure holiday: options include safaris, hot-air ballooning, trekking, mountain-biking and ski-mountaineering.

BY ROAD

From the UK, the main route from the French ferry ports runs south to Bordeaux and into Spain at Irun, west of the Pyrenees, then on to San Sebastian and Burgos. From there, you take the N-1 to Madrid and the N-IV to Bailén, continuing on the N-IV southwest to Cordoba then south again to Málaga, and west along the coast to the ferry at Algeciras. Allow three to four days of steady driving.

Driving time can be cut by using the long-distance car-ferry service from Plymouth to Santander in northern Spain (a 24-hour trip). From Santander, follow the N-623 to Burgos and proceed as described above.

BY RAIL

There is a direct rail service to Algeciras from Paris. Allow about two days for the full journey from London to Tangier. For details, contact British Rail at London Victoria, tel. (071) 834 2345.

The Inter-Rail Card, which permits 30 days of unlimited rail travel in participating European countries to people under 26, is valid for second-class travel on Moroccan railways and entitles the holder to a 30% discount on the Algeciras-Tangier ferry.

BY SEA

The main ferry port for Morocco is Algeciras in Spain, a half-hour bus trip from Gibraltar. From here, car and passenger ferries make around six crossings a day to Tangier (2 hours 30 minutes), and about 12 a day to Ceuta (1 hour 30 minutes). There are longer and less frequent car ferry crossings from Sète in France, and Almería and Màlaga in Spain, to Melilla in Morocco. For details, contact Southern Ferries, 179 Piccadilly, London W1V 9DB, tel. (071) 491 4986. Tickets for cars should be reserved well in advance.

For foot passengers only, there are also hydrofoil services on these routes, with faster crossing times of 1 hour to Tangier and 30 minutes to Ceuta, but they do not run in heavy weather.

WATER

Although tap water is considered to be safe in most parts of Morocco, you are recommended to avoid drinking it. Bottled mineral water is easily obtainable everywhere – Sidi Harazem and Sidi Ali are the most popular brands of still mineral water; Oulmès is carbonated.

WEIGHTS and MEASURES

Temperature

Length

Weight

grams	0	100	200	300	400	500	600	700	800	900	1 kg
ounces	0	4	8	12	1 lb	20	24	28	2 lb		

WOMEN TRAVELLERS

It is unfortunate but true that foreign women travelling in Morocco are often subject to harassment from local men. This can range from cat-calls and whistles to rude comments and bottom-pinching. A woman accompanied by a man is less likely to attract unwanted attention but is not immune. Having said all this, the majority of Moroccans are courteous and friendly, and will show you genuine hospitality.

The way you dress is all-important; shorts and a halter top are not a good idea (this does not apply to resorts like Agadir where beachwear is the norm, nor to downtown Casablanca and Rabat). The best strategy is to dress modestly in trousers, or preferably a long skirt, and a long-sleeved, loose-fitting top. Avoid eye contact with local men, and ignore any rude comments.

The best place to meet and talk to Moroccan women is in the local *hammam*, or public bath, where the atmosphere is friendly and relaxed. You will probably be deluged with all sorts of questions about your home country and your life there.

Y

YOUTH HOSTELS (*auberge de jeunesse*)

Morocco has only a dozen or so basic youth hostels, almost all of them in large cities. If you're planning to make use of youth hostels during your stay, contact your national youth hostel association before departure to obtain an international membership card. Further information and a full list of hostels in Morocco and worldwide are available from the **International Youth Hostel Federation** (IYHF), 9 Guessens Road, Welwyn Garden City, Herts AL8 6QW, United Kingdom; tel. (0707) 332 487.

Index

Where there is more than one set of references, the one in **bold** refers to the main entry. References in *italics* refer to an illustration.

135

Berlitz – pack the world in your pocket!